Lust

A musical

Book, music and lyrics by

The Heather Brothers

Based on William Wycherley's *The Country Wife*

Samuel French — London
New York - Toronto - Hollywood

ISBN 0 573 08098 4

Printed at Redwood Books, Trowbridge, Wiltshire.

LUST

First produced in London at the Theatre Royal Haymarket on 19th July, 1993, with the following cast:

Horner	Denis Lawson
Quack	Paul Leonard
Patient	Colin Marsh
Quack's Assistant	Janet Devenish
Footmen	Colin Marsh
	Stuart Pendred
Lady Fidget	Judith Paris
Sir Jasper	Anthony Dawes
Sparkish	Sean Wilton
Prudence	Janet Devenish
Squeamish	Karen-Jane Tomlinson
Dainty	Kate O'Sullivan
Dorilant	Andrew Nyman
Rudge	Tim Willis
Margery	Sophie Aldred
Pinchwife	Julian Curry
Harcourt	Mark Haddigan
Doxy	Janet Devenish
Gentlemen	Colin Marsh
	Stuart Pendred
Serving Girls	Janet Devenish
	Sarah Moyle
Alithea	Helen Hobson
Servant	Stuart Pendred
Chastity	Sarah Moyle
Hangman	Colin Marsh
Hangman's Wife	Sarah Moyle
Captain Jack	Stuart Pendred
Parson	Colin Marsh
Fiddler	Andrew Sherwood

Originally produced by Heathford Limited
By arrangement with Mario Lanfranchi and Cyril Humphris
Directed by Bob Carlton
Designed by Geoff Rose
Choreographed by Irving Davies
Orchestration by David Firman

SYNOPSIS OF SCENES AND MUSICAL NUMBERS

PROLOGUE

SCENE 1 A London courtyard
Song 1: "Lust" Company

SCENE 2 Quack's surgery
Song 2: "The Art of Deceiving" Quack, Horner

ACT I

SCENE 1 The orangery of a London house. Monday noon
Song 3: "Serve the Dog Right" Company
Song 4: "I Live for Love" Horner

SCENE 2 A busy London street. Monday 4 p.m.

SCENE 3 The tavern. Tuesday 3 p.m.
Song 5: "A Pox on Love and Wenching" Horner, Quack, Harcourt, Sparkish, Dorilant, Rudge
Song 6: "I Live for Love (Reprise)" Horner

SCENE 4 Pinchwife's lodgings. Tuesday 3.30 p.m.
Song 7: "Somewhere Out There" Margery

SCENE 5 Lady Fidget's boudoir. Tuesday 4 p.m.
Song 8: "Ladies of Quality" Lady Fidget, Squeamish, Dainty
Song 9: "Husbands Beware" Company

SCENE 6 Outside the theatre. Tuesday 6 p.m.
Song 10: "Why Did You Have to Come into My Life?" Harcourt, Alithea

SCENE 7 Pinchwife's lodgings. Tuesday 6.15 p.m.

SCENE 8 The quay. Tuesday 7 p.m.
Song 11: "What a Handsome Little Fellow" Company

Song 12: "Tyburn Jig" Company
Song 13: "Wait and See"/"Lust" Company

ACT II

SCENE 1 Various locations. Wednesday 10.45 a.m.
Song 14: "Lust" (Reprise) Company
Song 15: "Dear Sir" Pinchwife, Margery

SCENE 2 Horner's lodgings. Wednesday 11 a.m.
Song 16: "Ode to the One I Love" Horner
Song 17: "China" Company

SCENE 3 Pinchwife's lodgings. Wednesday 11.30 a.m.
Song 18: "Come Tomorrow" Alithea, Harcourt, Margery

SCENE 4 Horner's lodgings. Wednesday noon
Song 19: "A Little Time in the Country" Horner, Quack
Song 20: "The Master Class" Horner, Margery

SCENE 5 A street. Wednesday 12.30 p.m.

SCENE 6 Horner's lodgings. Wednesday 1 p.m.
Song 21: "One of You" Horner, Lady Fidget, Dainty, Squeamish
Song 22: "Vengeance" Company
Song 23: "The Master Class" (Reprise) Horner, Dainty, Lady Fidget, Squeamish, Margery
Song 24: "We Thank You"/"Lust" (Reprise) Company

Music available on hire from Samuel French Ltd

CHARACTERS

Horner, a handsome libertine
Quack, a physician
Pinchwife, a dour, middle-aged country gentleman
Margery Pinchwife, a voluptuous country girl
Sir Jasper Fidget, an aristocratic gentleman
Lady Fidget, an extremely haughty aristocrat
Mistress Dainty, Lady Fidget's sister, also haughty
Mistress Squeamish, an austere, aristocratic woman
Alithea Pinchwife, a placid, refined country lady
Harcourt, a young blade
Dorilant, a loud, bluff gentleman
Sparkish, a plump, effeminate fop
Fiddler, a street musician

Male Extra 1: **Rudge, Executioner, Parson**
Female Extra 1: **Mistress Prudence, Serving Wench, Hag**
Male Extra 2: **Footman, Captain Jack**
Female Extra 2: **Mistress Charity, Serving Wench**

The action takes place in various locations in London

Time — 1661

The action is continuous

The set, a courtyard, is a single structure which epitomizes London of the Restoration period. Various sections of the structure move to become different locations

PROLOGUE

Scene 1

A London courtyard

Quack enters in front of the tabs. He strikes the stage three times with his staff

Quack 'Tis the city of London, the year 1661. Charles the Second has been crowned. The Restoration has begun.

Two groups stand silhouetted, one of men and one of women. They are dressed in Puritan cloaks and hats

Quack clicks his fingers to start the song

During the first part of the song the groups converge and merge

Song 1: "Lust"

Company At last
The age has passed
Of closeted sexuality.
You've been denied
For far too long,
So cast aside
My merry throng,
The shackles of Puritan austerity.
Loosen your grip
And let your morals slip.

The Ladies slowly let their cloaks slip, revealing bare shoulders

And slip, and slip, and slip and slip and slip.
Come join with us in celebration
To the glorious restoration
Of the noblest urge bestowed on us.

Men Wholesome and healthy,

Women Frolicsome and carefree,
Company Good old-fashioned,
Earthy and robust
Lust!
Lust.
Ring the bells of Restoration.
Lust,
Put the merry back in England.
Dorilant Come gird up your loins
Sparkish And discard your truss.
Company Revel in healthy,
Frolicsome and carefree,
Good old-fashioned,
Earthy and robust
Lust!
Lust!

Lady Fidget, Mistress Squeamish and Mistress Dainty form a group C

Quack And so begins our tale of rabid infidelity
About a friend of mine whose forte was adultery.
The name of Horner was synonymous with lustful promiscuity and lechery.
To Horner, beauty, wit and youth were no prerequisite.
If it was female and it moved then he would roger it.
Dainty A-ha
Squeamish A-ha
Lady Fidget A-ha

The Ladies, jumping aside as though they have been goosed, reveal Horner lying languidly on the stage

Horner My exploits in the beds and boudoirs of the ladies of society
Ladies }
Horner } Were legend'ry.
Horner Yes they were legend'ry.
Quack With each new mistress it appeared his appetite increased.
He passed from conquest on to conquest like a rampant beast.
In stamina, inventiveness and robust vigour Horner reigned supreme.

Horner The greatest libertine
London had ever seen.

Quack Yet as his tally grew at what was an heroic pace
Among the men folk of the town a change had taken place.

Men (*suspiciously*) A-ha
A-ha
A-ha

Quack Their sense of envy turned to outrage with the knowledge
The next lady fair
To sample Horner's wares could easily be theirs.

Men My lady could be next to sample Horner's wares.

Quack Thus fired with righteous indignation,
Laced with porter and desperation,
Battle lines were drawn, stratagems discussed.

Men We must deny him, somehow nullify him.

Ladies, Horner Good old-fashioned earthy and robust lust.

Men He'll not make cuckolds out of us.

Ladies, Horner Lust.

Men We will watch him night and day, sir.

Ladies, Horner Lust.

Men Keep this cavalier at bay, sir.
We'll foil his foil and we'll parry his thrust.

Ladies, Horner Revel in healthy,
Frolicsome and carefree,
Good old-fashioned,
Earthy and robust
Lust.

Men He'll not make cuckolds out of us.

Ladies, Horner Wholesome and healthy robust lust!
Lust.

Men Us.

During the remainder of the song the men drag their ladies away from Horner

Ladies, Horner Lust.

Men Us.

Men and Ladies Lust. Us. Lust. Us. Lust. Us. Lust. Us.

Horner Wholesome and healthy robust (*he realizes he is alone*) ... lust.
Men You'll not make cuckolds out of us.
Horner Damn!

Horner is held in a spotlight

The sound of groans are heard. They form a cappella harmonies. The Lights come up to reveal:

SCENE 2

Immediately after. Quack's surgery

Quack is pulling out some poor unfortunate's tooth. A Hag assists him

Horner (*furiously*) Damn selfish hypocritical bigots! They have absolutely no regard for their ladies' pleasure! Absolutely no regard what-so-ever!
Quack Who sir?
Horner Those vindictive husbands, gout-ridden fathers and flatulent fiancés! That's who, sir! Blast their suspicious spying eyes!

The Man having his tooth pulled groans

(*Annoyed*) Do you mind, sir, we're trying to hold a conversation. (*To Quack*) It's a conspiracy, Quack. I swear they watch me night and day. I get within a stone's throw of a woman and her damned husband pops out of the woodwork as if by witchery.
Quack When do you sail for France?
Horner Tonight. Why?
Quack Perhaps when you return their vigilance will have lessened.
Horner Quack, you don't seem to comprehend the depth of their malicious persecution. You may not believe this and I tell you this in the strictest confidence as my physician and friend ... but this past month I have not had one single woman!
Patient Not one?
Horner Not one!

Shocked, Quack turns to Horner holding the pincers with the tooth

Quack Good grief man, your health'll suffer.

Horner My every ploy, every strategy is frustrated.
Quack Then you'll obviously have to change your strategy, sir ... Be more canny in your approach ... Maybe I could be of assistance.
Horner Good heavens, Quack! What could you possibly know about deception?
Quack (*offended*) Sir, I'm a physician... I practise it every day. (*He sings*)

Song 2: "The Art of Deceiving"

The art of deceiving,
Is making one believe in
That which in their heart of hearts
They want to be true.
All sense of reason disappears
When a man hears what he wants to hear.
A quirk of nature that's undoubtedly true.
That's why I, a physician,
Do as well as I do.

Patient (*groaning*) A-a-ah-ha-ha a-ha-ha a-ha-ha.

Quack
Tell a hag she is beautiful
A lovely sight to see,
Or a fool that he's a wit
And I'm sure they'll both agree.
Tell a dying man you can cure him
And he'll readily pay the fee.
For all men believe
What they want to believe.
So the key to your success, my friend,
Isn't intrigue or disguise.
Secret rendezvous
Or common-or-garden lies.
You must find what in their heart of hearts
These husbands want to hear,
And you'll be harvesting their fruit, my friend,
For many a lusty year.

Horner
So the art of deceiving
Is making one believe in
That which in their heart of hearts
They want to be true.

Quack
All sense of reason disappears
When a man hears what he wants to hear.

Both A quirk of nature that's undoubtedly true.
Quack That's why I, a physician,
And my brothers in religion,
Horner Not forgetting politicians,
Both Do as well as we/you do.

Quack You must find what in their heart of hearts
These husbands want to hear,
And you'll be harvesting their fruit, my friend,
Furrowing their fields, my friend.
Horner I'll be servicing their mares, my friend,
Both For many a lusty year.

Horner (*speaking; putting his arm around Quack's shoulder*) Quack, an idea ...

Horner exits

Quack (*singing*) With a plan conceived, Horner sailed for France.
While here husbands planned to repel his next advance.
But to their surprise on his return, 'twas said
After consulting with his surgeon,
(*Speaking*) My good self
He'd been confined to bed
(*Speaking*) Whereupon ...

Change into:

ACT I

Scene 1

The orangery of a London house. Monday at noon

Sir Jasper, Lady Fidget, Harcourt, Dorilant, Mistress Squeamish, Mistress Dainty, Sparkish, Mistress Charity, Mistress Prudence and Rudge are dancing. A Footman stands at the door. Quack crosses the stage

Quack (*singing*) A rumour, circulated round London town,
Made the gentlemen chuckle and the ladies frown.
'Twas said Horner's prowess had been negated.

(*Sitting*) Whilst in France he'd caught the pox and he'd been ——

All — castrated.

Song 3: "Serve the Dog Right"

Lady Fidget Have you heard about
Mister Horner?
It seems that honey-bee
Has lost its sting.
Sir Jasper I assure you it's true,
I heard it from his surgeon.
Sparkish That's one beau's bells
That'll no longer ring.
Ding dong.
Sir Jasper Ding ding.

Squeamish
Dainty We've just heard the news
That's spreading round Whitehall.
The prince of cuckoldom's
Reign's come to an end.
Dorilant He abdicated
Out of respect for the dead, ma'am.
The poor old fellow
Has lost his best friend.
Ding dong.
Rudge Ding ding.

Crowd Oh, yes,
Serve the dog right!
Dorilant I know I'll sleep easier in my bed tonight.
Crowd Oh, yes,
Serve the dog right!
Dorilant I know I'll sleep easier in my bed,
Since his gun's been spiked!
Sparkish Since his gun's been spiked!
Crowd Serve the dog right!

Footman (*speaking*) Master Horner.

There is a momentary silence as Horner enters

The music continues. All eyes follow him as he crosses to Quack and sits

Horner So, dear Quack, have you been busy on my behalf?

Quack Ay, I said you'd caught the pox whilst in Paris and on your return my remedy was not only a cure but an antidote for ever catching it in the future.

Horner But did they believe you?

Quack Without exception. (*Holding up a glass jar*) It's remarkable how convincing two pickled walnuts can be to the undiscerning eye.

Horner (*hurt; holding up the jar*) Pickled walnuts?

Noticing the jar, the dancers freeze and gasp

(*Singing; to Quack*) They'll never suspect poor mutilated me.
What husband would dream a eunuch could be
The cause of his wife's infidelity?
Such is my strategy.

Quack Thanks to my tale of your condition,
Horner I'm beneath contempt
Horner, Quack But above suspicion.
Thanks to our strategy
Horner They'll never suspect me.

The Crowd gather around Horner and sing

Squeamish Have you taken up
Bare-back riding?
It seems he's acquired
A peculiar gait.

Lady Fidget It appears French cuisine
Did not agree with Horner.
(*Staring at his crutch*) It's plain to see
You've lost a little weight.

Dorilant Pray, sir, while in France
Did you have your voice trained?
It certainly seems to have risen in pitch.

Sparkish If I were you, sir,
I'd have a word with your tailor.
You need your breeches
Taken in a stitch.

Ladies Ding dong.
Ding ding.

The Crowd break away laughing

Crowd Oh, yes,
Horner }
Quack } Oh, yes.
Crowd Serve the dog right.
Horner }
Quack } Serve them right.
Crowd I know I'll sleep easier in my bed tonight.
Oh, yes,
Horner }
Quack } Oh, yes,
Crowd Serve the dog right.
Horner }
Quack } Serve them right.
Men I know I'll sleep easier in my bed,
Since his gun's been spiked.
Horner }
Quack } Thanks to our strategy
Crowd Serve the dog right.
Horner They'll never suspect me.
So let them sneer,
Let them jeer,
At my apparent demise.
I assure you, dear Quack,
The phoenix will rise.

Crowd Serve the dog right!
Horner }
Quack } And rise.
Crowd Serve the dog right!
All Serve the dog/dogs right!

Sir Jasper, followed by the others, crosses to Horner

Sir Jasper Master Horner, sir!
Horner Sir Jasper.
Sir Jasper I must apologize for not having visited you since your return from France, Horner. But as they say, business always comes before pleasure with the wise.
Quack And the impotent, Sir Jasper.
Sir Jasper (*sniggering*) Ay, and the impotent, doctor.

The others snigger

May I present my Lady Fidget.

Lady Fidget offers Horner her hand to be kissed

Horner (*ignoring her hand; coolly*) Madam.
Sir Jasper Pray sir, will you not kiss my lady's hand?
Horner I will kiss no portion of any man's wife, sir. I have taken my eternal leave of the fairer ... sex.
Sir Jasper But sir, you know my wife.
Horner Indeed I do. She is a woman and consequently a monster.

There is a gasp from the others

Lady Fidget (*to the others*) It would appear the gelding also lost his manners whilst in France ... let us be gone from this rude fellow.
Horner You may as well, madam. I no longer have anything you desire.
Lady Fidget French capon. (*To the Ladies*) Come, ladies, I can no longer endure the sight of him.

Lady Fidget, followed by Squeamish and Dainty, moves away in a huff

Sir Jasper You must do me the honour of visiting my house, Horner. Please, I beseech you. Come dine with us and perhaps play a few hands of cards with my wife. (*He sniggers*) I take it you are still fit to play women at that game?
Horner See how they treat me, Quack? Like some superannuated stallion who's allowed to run, feed and whinny with the mares because he can do nothing else. Well, a pox on you, Sir Jasper, and your good lady wife. In fact, a pox on all womankind. I'm done with the lot of them and glad of it.
Quack Oh come, come, Horner. Don't be so sensitive, man. You can't blame Sir Jasper for taking advantage of your circumstances. It's as prudent for an intelligent husband to provide innocent diversions for his wife as it is to hinder her unlawful pleasures. Correct, Sir Jasper?
Sir Jasper Quite. And I'm nothing if I'm not intelligent.
Lady Fidget (*impatiently*) Sir Jasper!
Sir Jasper Coming, my dear. (*To Horner*) Your servant, sir.
Horner Sir.
Lady Fidget (*as she goes*) Foh!
Dainty / **Squeamish** } (*as they go*) Foh!

The Ladies exit

Sir Jasper (*as he goes*) Coming, my dear, coming ...

Sir Jasper and the Gentlemen exit after the Ladies

Horner moves downstage with Quack

Horner (*overjoyed*) My God, it's working. Sir Jasper, who before would never even have allowed me to cross his threshold, invites me to his house to play with his wife.
Quack At cards, sir.
Horner For the time being.
Quack Granted you've made yourself acceptable to the husbands, but by Lady Fidget's reaction you've made yourself unacceptable to the wives.
Horner Dear Quack, you may be an authority on the workings of the human body but I, sir, am an authority on the workings of the female mind. 'Tis only scandal they avoid, not men. Now I can be sure that she who shows an aversion to my condition as did our dear Lady Fidget loves the sport.
Quack I hope for your sake you are correct in your assumption, Horner.
Horner Time will tell.
Quack Indeed. Until tomorrow then.
Horner Adieu.
Quack (*as he goes*) Adieu.

Quack exits

The Lights fade, leaving Horner isolated

Horner So now I have the reputation of a eunuch, I have the privileges of one too. I can be seen in a lady's chamber in the morning, frolic with virgins before their parents and fiancés ... In short I have a permit to do as I will and believe me I will! (*He sings*)

Song 4: "I Live for Love"

I can see it now.
Candlelight reflected
On a milk white alabaster skin.
Midnight eyes,
Blue, brown, grey or green,
It doesn't matter — they'll be beckoning.

And that silhouette
So round and full.
Caught in the moonlight,
Promising the pleasures of the night,
The earthly delights of a clandestine rendezvous.
I live for love.
I live for love.
I live for love.
I live, I live, I live for love.
I live, I live, I live for love.

Some men lust for riches and gold.
Some men for the trappings of nobility.
Some men lust for power, I'm told.
But oh no,
Oh no,
Not me.
Not me.
I live for love.
I live for love.
I live for love.
I live, I live, I live for love.
I live, I live, I live for love.
I live, I live, I live for love.

Black-out

Scene 2

A busy London street. Monday 4 p.m.

Pinchwife and his wife Margery enter. She is wearing a cloak. Margery looks around in wonderment

Pinchwife (*hurrying her along*) Come, Margery, the theatre is this way.
Margery Don't rush me, husband. I want to see some sights. I must have something to tell my friends at home about.
Pinchwife Later, dearest. There will be time for that later. And stay close, madam.

Dorilant and Harcourt come out of one of the houses with a wench. Dorilant kisses her hand and flicks her a coin. They are about to leave when they notice Pinchwife

You're not in Hampshire now — this is London. These lecherous town jays'd ravish a lady as soon as look at her.

Dorilant (*calling*) Pinchwife.

Pinchwife (*seeing him*) Shitese! (*To Margery*) Keep yourself covered, madam. Keep yourself covered. (*Turning*) Dorilant. Harcourt.

Harcourt Dear friend.

Dorilant Good to see you, Pinchwife. I thought I recognized your crusty countenance.

Harcourt I take it you're in London for your sister's wedding, sir?

Pinchwife I'd hardly be here out of choice.

Dorilant Do I deduce from your tone, sir, you won't be staying with us long?

Pinchwife Not a moment longer than necessary, sir. I arrived this morning and I'll be returning to Hampshire the moment the ceremony's over.

Dorilant Ah, then you can't have heard about friend Horner ——

Pinchwife (*interrupting*) I'll trouble you not to mention that whore-monger's name in my presence, Dorilant, unless it's to announce his death.

Harcourt Come now, Pinchwife. You don't still hold a grudge, surely?

Pinchwife Certain grievances do not diminish with time, sir. I bid you good day. Walk on, madam, walk on.

Pinchwife and Margery exit. Quack enters

Dorilant The old toad's still as cantankerous as ever.

Harcourt (*laughing*) Pinchwife must be the only fellow in London not to have heard of Horner's condition.

Dorilant Ah Quack, have you seen Horner?

Quack I believe he's meeting you "gentlemen" at the theatre.

Dorilant Is he? Then we'd best hurry — the play will have started.

Harcourt and Dorilant exit

Quack (*singing*) Friend Horner's appearance at the theatre that night
They say was met with ribald delight.

Laughter from off stage

The raillery lasted throughout the play
And continued at the tavern on the following day.

Change to:

Scene 3

The tavern. The following afternoon. Tuesday 3 p.m.

From the darkness the sound of a crowd is heard. A fiddle is playing

The Lights come up to reveal Harcourt, Dorilant, Sparkish, Rudge and Male Company sitting at a tavern table. Quack joins them

Sparkish I trust Horner's appearance at the theatre last night has hardened him against a future of ridicule. I must say I baited him unmercifully, did I not?
Dorilant Indeed you did, Sparkish. Your howls of derision would have mortified a lesser man.
Harcourt Poor fellow. He bore it most bravely.

He places the jar of walnuts on the table much to the amusement of all

Quack Surely the ladies pitied him?
Sparkish Pshaw, sir. What ladies do you mean? I find the whores never pity a man when he's unable to provide the means.
Rudge Ay, even if he did lose it in their service.
Sparkish And as for the ladies of quality, they say all who dally with common women deserve as much.
Harcourt Can you imagine what the poor fellow's going through? It's bad enough a mere mortal losing his tackle ... But Horner?
Dorilant It's tantamount to Michelangelo losing his chisel.
Sparkish (*picking up the pickling jar with the walnuts*) Personally I'd rather have lost me sight.
Dorilant Really? For all the use you make of your appendages, Sparkish, I'd hardly have thought you'd know they were missing.

The others laugh as a Wench arrives with drinks

Sparkish Harcourt, dear friend, after we've visited my betrothed, perhaps you'd care to accompany us to the theatre and be my guest for dinner.
Harcourt You are most generous, sir.
Quack Beware of Sparkish's generosity, Harcourt.
Dorilant Indeed. The rogue still owes me for the last meal I was his "guest" at.
Sparkish Gentlemen, gentlemen. I admit I have been somewhat embarrassed of late, but I assure you before the week's out my debts will be honoured. Come tomorrow my coffers will be overflowing. Overflowing.

Dorilant (*bored*) Yes, the dowry, Sparkish ... We know.
Sparkish (*smugly*) Five thousand guineas. Not bad for an hour's work.
Dorilant Ay, and a lifetime of regret. Can you imagine having Pinchwife as a brother-in-law?
Quack Though why anyone'd pay Sparkish to marry them's beyond me. I'd thought it'd be the other way round.

The others laugh

Sparkish I'll have you know, sir, I'm considered a fine catch.
Dorilant So is a trout, Sparkish, but I'm damned if I'd marry one.

The others laugh

Horner enters

Harcourt Horner.
Horner (*joining them*) Gentlemen.
Dorilant Ah, no-ball friend.
Sparkish When you failed to turn up at the coffee house this morning we thought perhaps you'd thrown yourself into the Thames.
Horner Why on earth should I do that?
Harcourt Come now, Horner, there's no need to put on a front for us, sir.
Horner Front?
Sparkish (*holding up the pickling jar*) Ay, sir, a front.
Quack (*snatching the jar*) A moment's indiscretion, Horner. I apologize.
Horner Oh, you mean my condition? It may be hard for you rutting stags to believe but I thank providence for my condition. You see before you a happy, contented man.
Dorilant Oh come now, sir.
Horner It is true, Dorilant. Since I lost my sting I have discovered there are finer things in life than pursuing and bedding another man's wife. (*He sings*)

Song 5: "A Pox on Love and Wenching"

Since I've been purged of the urge to procreate,
I'm able for the first time in my life to appreciate
The beauty of everyday things,
And the absolutely, inexplicably, extraordinary
Pleasure that pursuing them brings.
And so today
I can honestly say,

Thank God I've acquired the ultimate cure
And no longer enticed by the sexual lure.
Thank God I can say with no fear of contention,
A pox,
A pox,
On love and on wenching.
A pox.

Others A pox?
Horner A pox.
Others A pox?
Horner On love and on wenching.

Out of the corner of his eye Horner sees a Maid clearing a table. Her ample rear sways as she works

(*Mesmerized*) Many manly pleasures in the country are found,
But the greatest by far is riding to hounds.
Great care should be taken when selecting a steed,
My personal preference is for comfort not speed.
First you mount your filly with a tally-ho!
Dig in your heels and away you go.
The trick's to keep the starting pace slow and steady,
Then increase your speed, you'll know she's ready
When you feel her quivering between your knees,
Responding urgently to every squeeze.
By gad, it's fun!

Men } **Horner** } By gad, it's fun!
Horner You are as one.
Men You are as one.
Horner And then you're urging, surging,
Plunging, lunging,
Bouncing, striving, thrusting, driving,
Onwards, onwards, ever faster!
Faster, faster, damn you, faster ...

Quack (*realizing Horner is getting carried away*) Whoa!

Horner comes to his senses and, to conceal his growing excitement, snatches up his cane and starts morris dancing. The others join in

Horner Thank God I've acquired the ultimate cure.
Men Ultimate cure.

Horner And no longer enticed by the sexual lure.
Men Sexual lure.
Horner Thank God I can say with no fear of contention,
A pox.
Others A pox.
Horner A pox.
Others A pox.
Horner On love and on wenching.
A pox.
Others A pox.
Horner A pox.
Others A pox.
Horner On love and on wenching.

You city fellows may scoff at those who work on the land.
But I find rustic life both merry and grand.
Milking your first heifer is a joy to recall.
(*Dreamily*) Her bountiful young udders so rounded and full.
First you move in close then slip your hands below,
Take a firm grip and away you go.
The trick's to keep your starting pace slow and steady.
Then increase your speed, you'll know she's ready
When you feel her quivering against your knees
And lowing gratefully at every squeeze.
By gad it's fun.
Others By gad it's fun.
Horner You are as one.
Others You are as one.
Horner (*losing himself again*) And then you're stroking, coaxing,
Grasping, clasping,
Pressing, seizing, tugging, squeezing,
Pulling, teasing, rubbing, kneading,
Kneading, kneading, screaming, pleading,
Harder, harder, ever faster.
Faster, faster, damn you, faster ...
Quack Whoa!

Horner Thank God I've acquired the ultimate cure.
Others Ultimate cure.
Horner And no longer enticed by the sexual lure.
Others Sexual lure.
Horner Thank God I can say with no fear of contention,
A pox.

Others A pox.
Horner A pox.
Others A pox.
Horner On love and on wenching.
A pox.
Others A pox.
Horner A pox.
Others A pox.
All On love, love, love, love,
A pox on love and on wenching!
Pox! Pox! Pox! Pox!

Pinchwife enters

Sparkish spots him

Pinchwife Gentlemen.
Sparkish Pinchwife! Come and join us, sir.

Pinchwife crosses to them

Pinchwife (*bowing*) Gentlemen.
Horner By your slovenly dress and (*he grimaces*) fragrant aroma, Pinchwife, I deduce you've just come up from the country.
Pinchwife (*ignoring Horner*) Sparkish, I came to speak of the dowry but I see you are otherwise engaged. Good-day, gentlemen.
Dorilant Not so fast, Pinchwife. What's this Sparkish tells us about you being married?
Pinchwife That is correct.
Rudge The next thing we'll hear is his wife's taken a lover and made him a cuckold.
Dorilant I must say I did not expect an old whoremaster who knew the town women so well to take a wife.
Pinchwife I married no town woman, sir. Mine is a country wife. At least in the country we know our women are unsullied.
Quack Oh come, come, Pinchwife! I've known a fellow to catch the clap as far afield as Wales.
Dorilant There are magistrates and chaplains in the country too, are there not?
Harcourt Not to mention coachmen and gardeners.
Pinchwife (*weary*) I see town wit has not improved in my absence.
Horner Oh I'd say it greatly improved in his absence.

Dorilant Your wife, sir ... She's handsome and young?

Pinchwife No, no, no. Austere best describes my plain, scrawny, spindle-shanked Margery.

Quack Then she must be rich.

Pinchwife In virtue only. Being ugly, she'll remain faithful. Being ill-bred, she'll hate conversation ... and as for intelligence, I've always been of the opinion he's a fool that marries but he's a greater one that does not marry a fool.

Horner Well obviously marriage hasn't cured the man of whoring. (*To Pinchwife*) We saw you last night at the theatre sitting in the middle gallery amongst the whores with the most devilishly pretty wench.

Dorilant Indeed we did, sir.

Harcourt Devilishly pretty.

Pinchwife (*flustered*) Ahh ... yes ... well ...

Harcourt What? Blushing? For having been seen with a wench?

Dorilant I warrant that was no wench he was with but his wife!

Horner (*suddenly interested*) His wife? (*His attitude to Pinchwife changes dramatically to one of acute friendliness*)

Pinchwife No, no, no.

Quack It was his wife! Men are more ashamed to be seen with their wives in public than a whore.

Horner (*to the others*) She was exceedingly pretty.

Dorilant So exceedingly pretty, in fact, Horner told me he fell madly in love with her even at that distance.

Pinchwife Well I can assure Mr Horner he's like never to be nearer to her!

Horner Nearer? Why on earth should I wish to get any nearer?

Pinchwife Don't play the innocent with me, sir. I know you of old.

Horner Ahh, Lady Elizabeth? That was a misunderstanding.

Pinchwife (*interrupting*) We were betrothed, damn your eyes!

Dorilant He was merely breaking her in for you, Pinchwife.

Quack, Rudge and Harcourt laugh

Pinchwife (*ignoring them; to Horner*) You made a fool of me once, sir, but never again!

Horner Your fears are unfounded. Quack, Quack, tell him of my condition.

Quack Mister Horner is ——

Dorilant (*interrupting*) In prime condition, sir. I wager a guinea he's had your wife before the week's out.

Horner He jests.

Dorilant Two guineas.

The others laugh

Pinchwife Sparkish, I'll expect you at my lodgings later.
Dorilant Make that six guineas, sir.

Pinchwife turns to leave

Horner Pinchwife, wait! (*He grabs his arm*) You don't understand ——
Pinchwife (*breaking free; violently*) I understand you all too well, Horner. You are a debauched licentious fornicator, sir. Well, be warned — come sniffing around my wife and you'll regret it. Do I make myself clear? If you value your life keep away from my wife Margery.

Pinchwife exits in a rage to the amusement of all except Horner

The Lights fade, leaving Horner and Quack isolated

Horner (*salaciously to Quack*) So it was Margery. Margery Pinchwife. Fresh and ripe from the country. (*He sings*)

Song 6: "I Live for Love" (Reprise)

I can see her now,
Plump young breasts atremble
With the passion of her inner fire.
Sturdy limbs,
Blushing cheeks aflame
With all the longing of her heart's desire.
And those rounded hips
So soft and full.
Margery Pinchwife,
I promise you the pleasures of the night,
The earthly delights
Of a clandestine rendezvous.

Smiling, Quack exits unnoticed by Horner who is in a world of his own

I live for love.
I live for love.
I live for love.
I live, I live, I live for love.
I live, I live, I live for love.

Black-out

Scene 4

Pinchwife's lodgings. Tuesday 3.30 p.m.

Margery Pinchwife is combing her sister-in-law Alithea's hair. Alithea is thirty years old, placid and refined

Margery I don't think my husband's smiled once since we arrived yesterday, Alithea. I can't understand it. He seems so vexed.

Alithea He has a lot on his mind, Margery, what with my wedding to Master Sparkish.

Margery (*not listening*) And why he wouldn't let me wear my best gown to the theatre last night's beyond me. Do you know he insisted we sat in the middle gallery amongst the coarse and common people? He wouldn't let me near the gentry ...

Alithea Yes, dear ...

Margery He told me none but the naughty wicked women sat there whom they (*she giggles*) toused and moused, rumpled and toyed with.

Alithea Yes, but how did you find the play?

Margery Oh, most wearisome: but I liked the actors hugely.

Alithea Heavens, child, if my brother heard you say that you'd never set foot inside a theatre again.

Margery But it's the truth, Alithea. They are the prettiest of men.

Alithea Looks aren't everything, Margery. There are other qualities far more deserving of a lady's admiration.

Margery That's as it may be, sister, but it don't stop my heart fluttering at the prospect of seeing those pretty actor men on stage again tonight.

Alithea laughs in spite of herself

Pinchwife enters in a furious mood, slams the door and hands Margery his coat

Margery (*excited*) Honey-bud, you're home! ... We'd best leave immediately or we'll be late for the theatre.

Pinchwife (*peering out the window*) You're not going!

Margery (*taken aback*) What d'you mean, honey-bud?

Pinchwife Are you deaf as well as stupid, madam? Exactly that. You're not going to the theatre!

Margery (*close to tears*) But why?

Pinchwife I have my reasons.

Margery But I was so looking forward to it ... Please.

Pinchwife No!
Margery Honey-bud ——
Pinchwife No! And that's an end to it!

Margery exits with the coat

Alithea Why shouldn't she go?
Pinchwife (*turning to Alithea*) Why? I'll tell you why, sister.

Margery enters and overhears the conversation

Because one of the lewdest fellows in London saw the minx at the theatre last night and told me to my face he was in love with her. That's why! Satisfied?
Margery Really? Who was it, honey-bud? I'm most beholding to him.
Pinchwife Beholding ... ? To a man who would ruin you?
Margery If he loved me, why would he ruin me?
Pinchwife Cretinous simpleton.
Alithea I would never allow a man to speak to me like that.
Pinchwife Which no doubt is why it's taken so long to find you a husband — even with a dowry of five thousand guineas. You don't know your place in the world, madam. You are a woman and by definition subservient to man.
Alithea (*furiously*) I swear, brother, if I were your wife I'd poison your food.
Pinchwife If you were my wife, sister, I'd willingly eat it.

Glaring at him, Alithea turns on her heel and exits

Margery Is he pretty?
Pinchwife What ... ?
Margery The gallant that loves me ... Is he pretty?
Pinchwife (*his eyes to heaven*) God preserve us.

A Servant enters

Servant Master Sparkish and a gentleman, sir.
Margery Oh Jeminy! Could it be him, honey-bud?
Pinchwife (*to Margery; panicking*) What ... ? Quick! Into the bedchamber.
Margery But honey-bud ...

Pinchwife exits, pushing Margery into the bedroom

Pinchwife (*as they go*) In, baggage. In!

As Pinchwife closes the door behind him Sparkish and Harcourt enter

Sparkish I first met Alithea at Pinchwife's estate in Hampshire, and though plain she is of good rustic stock.

Alithea enters

Ah, Alithea my dear, may I introduce Mister Harcourt. He is one of those who will dance at our wedding tomorrow.

Harcourt and Alithea are attracted to each other

Harcourt Madam.
Alithea Sir.
Sparkish Well Harcourt, do you approve? ... Harcourt ... ?

Harcourt does not react

Harcourt?
Harcourt (*confused*) Sorry?
Sparkish Do you approve my choice?
Harcourt Yes, yes indeed. You have my envy, sir.
Sparkish Oh splendid! I do so love to be envied. It gives me as much pleasure as counting my money in front of the poor.
Harcourt In truth, I wish had a mistress that differed in nothing but her engagement to you.
Alithea Mister Sparkish has often told me his acquaintances were all wits and jesters — now I find it so.
Sparkish No, no, by the universe, madam, he does not jest. He is the most honest of fellows. I am sure he admires you extremely. Is that not so, sir?
Harcourt Indeed. Though I concede that never before have I envied any man about to marry.
Alithea Yes, I heard town gentlemen had an aversion to marriage, Mister Harcourt. That they loathe it almost as much as work.
Harcourt Madam, I have never loathed marriage because up until this moment marriage was never a threat to me. But now I confess if it was in my power I'd break this match.
Alithea Would you be so unkind to me?
Sparkish (*superciliously*) Pshaw! Madam. It has nothing to do with unkindness to you — it is out of sympathy for me. Us town wits mourn our brothers about to marry as though they had developed the first signs of plague. Is that not so, Harcourt?

Harcourt is staring mesmerized at Alithea

Harcourt!

Pause

(*To Alithea*) Madam, inform your brother it's time we were leaving.

Pause

(*Clapping his hands*) Come, come, madam.

Alithea (*annoyed by his tone; looking at him coldly*) You are a little free with your instructions, sir.

Sparkish Nay, madam. Merely having proof of your obedience.

Alithea I'll be a wife, sir, but no man's servant.

Alithea exits

Harcourt I envy you your good fortune, Sparkish.

Sparkish (*smugly*) I'm sure you do, sir. Five thousand guineas.

Harcourt No, no, you misunderstand me ——

Pinchwife enters, followed by Margery and Alithea

Pinchwife (*as he enters*) Gentlemen.

Sparkish Ah Pinchwife, Margery, let us away to the theatre.

Pinchwife My wife will not be attending the play.

Margery Honey-bud ——

Pinchwife (*interrupting*) She is unwell.

Sparkish (*concerned*) I trust your lady's *malaise* will not affect the wedding arrangements.

Pinchwife No, no, no, she's just a trifle fatigued from the journey.

Sparkish (*insincerely*) My condolences, madam. Still time and Wycherley wait for no man. Pinchwife, your hand. Harcourt, lead on with Alithea.

Harcourt My pleasure, sir.

Harcourt takes Alithea's hand and they exit

Sparkish (*as he exits*) Now about the dowry, Pinchwife.

Pinchwife (*as he exits*) Yes, about the dowry. On reflection I consider five thousand guineas somewhat excessive. (*He turns to poke his head back around the door. To Margery*) Be warned, madam: not one step outside these lodgings.

He exits

Margery (*breathlessly*) Oh Jeminy, to think a town gentleman loves me. Me, a homely country girl. (*She sings*)

Song 7: "Somewhere Out There"

Somewhere out there,
My love is waiting.
Anticipating
His first meeting with me.
When I close my eyes,
In my mind I can see
My lover coming,
Coming to me.

She mimes out her fantasy

Hark, is that footsteps
I hear on the stair?
I open the door
And my lover stands there.
So bold and so gallant,
So pretty, so grand.
He bows and I curtsy,
He kisses my hand.
How I blush when he whispers
Sweet nothings in my ear.
My poor heart beats so loudly
I'm sure he will hear.
As his strong arms enfold me,
I rest my head on his chest.
Then his lips brush my cheek
With the softest caress.

Somewhere out there,
My love is waiting.
Anticipating
His first meeting with me.
When I close my eyes,
In my mind I can see
My lover coming,
Coming to me.

He smiles so sweetly
My heart starts to race.
I cannot resist his
Rough manly embrace.
I feel his pulse quicken,
His breath comes in gasps.
His body starts shaking
As he loosens my clasp.
While one hand explores me
The other bolts the door.
Then removing his breeches,
He throws me to the floor.
As he bears down upon me
There's lust in his eyes.
I know it's pointless resisting,
He won't be denied.

Somewhere out there
That rogue is scheming,
Salaciously dreaming
Of his meeting with me.
Awfully sinful,
Wicked thoughts fill his head.
How I wish,
Oh, how I wish,
That brute was ...
(*Dreamily*) Here in my bed.

(*With a sigh*) Oh Jeminy.

Black-out

SCENE 5

Lady Fidget's boudoir. Tuesday 4 p.m.

Lady Fidget, Dainty and Squeamish are playing cards

Squeamish To think Master Horner's as harmless a man now as ever came out of Italy with a high voice almost beggars belief.

Lady Fidget But it is still nonetheless true, cousin. The fellow is without doubt *functuous officio*.

Dainty Divine justice.

Lady Fidget Indeed, sister. The Lord giveth and the Lord taketh away.

Dainty (*sniggering*) Lady Fidget, really!

Squeamish Mind you, if the truth be told I wager there's a few ladies in London tonight mourning the loss.

Lady Fidget Yes, well, I'm of the opinion, cousin, that any lady of breeding who sullies the honour of the ladies of her class by consorting with fellows of such scurrilous reputation deserves to be pilloried unmercifully.

Dainty Quite right, sister.

Squeamish Indeed, 'tis our duty as custodians of propriety to uphold the morals of the ladies of our class.

Lady Fidget Quite so. Our God-given duty, cousin.

Dainty (*putting down her cards*) Ombre.

Lady Fidget (*topping her*) Ombre.

Lady Fidget takes the money

Song 8: "Ladies of Quality"

Ladies We three
Ladies of quality
Must lead the fight against
Moral decay.
Lady Fidget Moral decay.
Dainty Moral decay.
Squeamish Moral decay.
Ladies We must be forever vigilant.
Lady Fidget Forever very vigilant.
Ladies Unflinchingly intolerant
Of those who stray.

Lady Fidget Has anyone heard anything of any lady of quality?
Any idle bit of tittle-tattle that smacks of infidelity?
Dainty Any indiscretion?
Squeamish Sexual *faux pas*?
Lady Fidget *Ménage-à-trois*? Yah?
Can anyone recall
Any juicy bit of scandal at all?
Dainty I can!
Squeamish And I!
Lady fidget Me too.
Dainty (*to Squeamish*) After you, dear.
Squeamish No, dear. After you.
Dainty Well, yesterday at half-past three

I saw a certain lady of quality
In St John's Wood.

Squeamish looks apprehensive

Lady Fidget Up to no good?
Dainty Doing what no lady of quality should.
Not even with her husband,
Let alone a common coachman.

From Squeamish's expression it was obviously her

Lady Fidget No!
Dainty Yes!
Lady Fidget In broad daylight?
Dainty 'Twas not a pretty sight, I can assure you.
Lady Fidget Shame! Shame!
Tell us the hussy's name
That we may vilify her!

Squeamish is dying a thousand deaths

Dainty Woe, woe,
I would if I could
But I can't
For I did not recognize her.
Squeamish You don't know her name?
Dainty No.
Squeamish (*relieved*) Oh, what a shame,
For I'd most certainly have crucified her.

Dainty Who's next to tell her news?
Lady Fidget (*to Squeamish*) After you, dear.
Squeamish No, dear, after you.
Lady Fidget I saw a certain lady
Indulging in debauchery and lechery.
Squeamish Oh, how obscene!
Lady Fidget In the extreme!
Spec'lly as her rutting ground was Paddington Green.

From Dainty's expression it was obviously her

Dainty Surely her companion
Could've been the lady's husband?
Lady Fidget One might,
But not all three.
Squeamish My God, she must be ambidextrous!
Shame! Shame!
Tell us the doxy's name
That we may ridicule her.

Dainty is dying a thousand deaths

Lady Fidget Woe, woe,
I wish that I could.
But alas,
Three naked bodies obscured her.
Dainty You don't know her name?
Lady Fidget Sorry.
Dainty (*relieved*) Oh, what a shame,
For I'd most certainly have ostracized her!

Squeamish While weekending at Lord Delaware's,
Remember, Lady Fidget, you were there,
I chanced upon the gazebo.
Dainty Gazebo?

Lady Fidget looks uncomfortable

Squeamish And there on the floor with her paramour

Lady Fidget looks decidedly ill

Dainty (*eagerly*) Yes? Yes?
Squeamish Was a lady playing at heave-ho.

Dainty looks confused

Dainty Heave-ho?
Squeamish You know, (*she gestures*)
Raise the mainsail and away you go.
Dainty (*with growing realization*) Oh! Oh! Oh!
Shame! Shame!
Tell us the doxy's name,
That we may vilify her — nay crucify her.

Squeamish Woe, woe,
I wish that I could,
But her long auburn tresses obscured her.

Pause. They turn and look at Lady Fidget

Lady Fidget (*encouraging the others to join in*)
We three
Ladies of quality
Ladies Must lead the fight against
Moral decay.
Lady Fidget Moral decay.
Dainty Moral decay.
Squeamish Moral decay.
Ladies We must be forever vigilant.
Lady Fidget Forever very vigilant.
Ladies Unflinchingly intolerant
On those who stray.
And ev'ry day,
In ev'ry way,
We'll make them pay,
And pay, and pay, and pay, and pay.
Yes, we three ladies of virtue and fidelity,
Will make them pay!

Sir Jasper and Horner enter

Sir Jasper Ah, my lady ... Come along, Horner, this way.

Lady Fidget (*seeing Horner; aghast*) What do you mean by bringing him here? (*To the Ladies*) Let us retire, ladies.

Sir Jasper No, no, stay dear ... To tell you the naked truth ——

Lady Fidget (*interrupting*) Sir Jasper! I'll not have you use such a lewd word as "naked" in my presence.

Sir Jasper Yes, yes, quite right ... sorry m'dear ... Unfortunately you see, the thing is I have business at Whitehall, and though it grieves me sorely alas I cannot make up the fourth at cards. Therefore I would have you ——

Lady Fidget (*interrupting*) Play with him? Never!

Horner If I'd known this was the reason you asked me to accompany you, Sir Jasper, I'd never have left the coffee-house. (*He bows*) If you'll excuse me, ladies.

Sir Jasper (*taking Horner's arm*) Come, come, man. Surely you don't wish to avoid the sweet society of womankind? That sweet, soft, gentle creature made for man's companion.

Horner My spaniel too is a soft, gentle creature and has all the womanly tricks. It can fawn, lie down, snap at your friends, make your bed hard, give you fleas and mange ... The only difference is of the two, the spaniel is the more faithful animal.

Squeamish Insolent brute!

Dainty Odious beast!

Lady Fidget (*outraged*) The man's a mortified castrated ram!

Sir Jasper (*in mock outrage*) Horner! For shame! Women must have some redeeming qualities, sir. After all, your mother was a woman. (*Taking him aside*) Actually it was your well-being that concerned me, sir. As you have no lady of your own to coddle you, why not use mine?

Horner No.

Sir Jasper You could eat at the house. Come and go as you please.

Horner I think not.

Sir Jasper But Horner ——

Horner No, no.

Sir Jasper But ... but ... but you see, sir ——

Horner (*interrupting*) I told you, sir, I have taken my eternal leave of the fairer ... (*he indicates the Ladies*) those.

Sir Jasper Very well, I'll be frank with you.

Horner When all else fails, tell the truth.

Sir Jasper Exactly. I've heard that a certain gentleman has designs on me good lady wife ...

Horner I fail to see what this has to do with me.

Sir Jasper Horner, dear friend, I need someone I can trust to chaperon her.

Horner Ahhh, I see.

Sir Jasper looks pleased with himself

Sir Jasper Come sir, say you will ... Please.

Horner (*pondering*) We-e-ell ...

Sir Jasper Please, for my sake.

Horner Oh very well, Sir Jasper, for your sake ... and your sake alone I acquiesce.

Sir Jasper Oh splendid! (*He crosses to Lady Fidget*) Madam, you're always complaining you never have enough card players you can cheat ——

Lady Fidget (*interrupting*) Beat! ... And the answer is no.

Sir Jasper I take it you are aware that friend Horner's the worst card player in the country?

Lady Fidget The worst ...?

Sir Jasper Without doubt. And what is more, his losses are legendary. Madam, the fool is ripe for the picking.

Lady Fidget Indeed? (*To the Ladies*) Then I will make this French capon pay for his coarse buffoonery of the noblest sex.

Sir Jasper Bravo. Serve the dog right.
Lady Fidget After all, money makes up for all other wants in a man.
Sir Jasper (*ushering Horner to Lady Fidget*) Come, Horner, my Lady wishes to play. Therefore I will leave you to your business pleasure and go to my pleasure business with peace of mind. When I return we will all go together to bid farewell to Captain Jack.

Sir Jasper exits

Horner Well ladies, shall we play?
Lady Fidget (*as she exits*) Foh!
Dainty (*as she exits*) Foh!
Squeamish (*as she exits*) Foh!
Horner (*as he exits*) Foh!

They all exit

Black-out. There is a flash of lightning

A spot picks out Quack

Song 9: "Husbands Beware"

Quack A shadow crossed the moon.
The hungry wolf has left its lair.
Its approach is unexpected,
Its quarry unprotected.
I warn husbands to beware.

Lights pick out the singers

The maestro's at the gate.
Seductive music fills the air.
That sly counterfeit castrato
Will soon play passionato
With your precious lady fair.
I warn husbands to beware.
Husbands take care.

A spot picks out Horner and Squeamish DL. *They sing*

Squeamish You made yourself a social outcast?
A thing to be despised?

Horner Madam, your honour and reputation
Is paramount in my eyes.
Squeamish And you're the same man that went to France?
As perfect as before?
Horner As perfectly perfect, madam,
Of that you can be sure.
Squeamish And it was me you did this for?
Horner It was you, Mistress Squeamish,
I did this for.

Music continues under as Dorilant enters

Dorilant (*speaking*) Horner, about my fiancée Mistress Squeamish. I have pressing business tomorrow and wondered if you would keep an eye on her for me.
Horner What are friends for, Dorilant? (*To Squeamish*) Madam, I seem to recall you enjoyed an early morning ride.
Squeamish Indeed. There is nothing quite so invigorating as a good gallop.
Horner In that case I'll call for you at nine. I'll stable the horse and come up the backway.
Squeamish Backway, frontway, I'll be ready and waiting.
Horner Ah yes!
Dorilant What my lady lacks in finesse she more than makes up with enthusiasm.

Horner exits

Squeamish Tally-ho.

Dorilant exits

A spot picks out Dainty DR. *She sings*

Dainty You made yourself a social outcast?
A thing to be despised?

Horner rushes on and sings

Horner Madam, your honour and reputation
Is paramount in my eyes.
Dainty And you're the same man that went to France?
As perfect as before?

Horner As perfectly perfect, madam,
Of that you can be sure.
Dainty And it was me you did this for?
Horner It was you, dear mistress — er ...
Dainty Dainty.
Horner I did this for.

Rudge enters and joins them

Rudge (*speaking*) Horner, my lady has developed a sudden penchant for porcelain and informs me that you are something of an expert on the subject.

Horner Well ... Yes, I suppose I am.

Rudge In that case, sir, I wondered if perhaps you could find time to instruct her on the finer points.

Horner Why certainly, Rudge. (*To Dainty*) Come to my lodgings tomorrow morning, madam. I'll try not to disappoint you.

Dainty Oh, I'm quite sure you'll rise to the occasion. Ten o'clock sir?

Rudge exits

Horner looks across at Squeamish. Noticing his glance, she smiles and, using her fan as a crop, strikes her rump as a rider would his mount

Horner (*to Dainty*) Best make that quarter-past, Mistress Wallop... Gallop ...

Dainty Dainty.

Horner (*as he exits*) What else.

Horner exits

A spot picks out Lady Fidget DC. *She sings*

Lady Fidget You made yourself a social outcast?
A thing to be despised?

Horner rushes on and sings to Quack

Horner Madam your honour ——

(*He realizes it is Quack; speaking*) Shitese! (*He rushes across to Lady Fidget and sings*)

Madam, your honour and reputation
Is paramount in my eyes.

Lady Fidget And you're the same man that went to France?
As perfect as before?

Horner As perfectly perfect, madam,
Of that you can be sure.

Lady Fidget And it was me you did this for?

Horner It was you, dear Lady Fidget,
I did this for.

Sir Jasper enters

Sir Jasper (*speaking*) Ah Horner, I hate to impose, but my lady's desperate to buy china tomorrow and I've been recalled to Whitehall.

Horner (*interrupting*) Bring her to my lodgings tomorrow morning, Sir Jasper. I'm sure I'll be able to find something to interest her from my private collection.

Sir Jasper Ah, splendid.

Lady Fidget As I recall you have an especially exquisite piece.

Horner Indeed and I've been saving it just for you, madam.

Lady Fidget Shall we say eleven o'clock tomorrow, sir?

Horner That will be my pleasure.

Quack (*singing; mocking the husbands*) Roll up husbands one and all.
Hear my call. Hear my call.
You're all invited to the cuckolds' ball.
Would-be cuckolds one and all.

City fops, to the manor born,
You've been warned. You've been warned.
You may laugh and you may scorn.
But you'll soon be wearing cuckold's horns.
Come take your turn with the cuckold's horns.

The Gentlemen encourage Horner to dance with their ladies. They clap, cheer, etc.

Company The devil's at the door.
Your lady's virtue to ensnare.
That illicit midnight caller
Is threat'ning to enthrall her.
He's warning husbands to beware.
Warning husbands to beware.

The thief is in the house.
A stealthy footstep on the stair.
Seeking out the family treasure
To plunder at his leisure.
Warning husbands to beware
Warning husbands to beware.
Warning husbands, husbands, husbands
Warning husbands, husbands
Husbands
Take care!

Cross-fade to:

Scene 6

Outside the theatre. Tuesday 6 p.m.

Harcourt enters

Song 10: "Why Did You Have to Come into My Life"

Harcourt Why did she have to come into my life
Turning my head like wine
Weaving a spell around my poor heart
Turning my head like wine
Summer wine.

Music continues under the following

Sparkish, Alithea and Pinchwife enter

Sparkish Us wits ... we love a good jest, do we not, Pinchwife? We were somewhat bold with that actor fellow.

Pinchwife Indeed we were, sir. Indeed we were.

Alithea I always thought one went to a play to laugh at the author's wit, not one's own.

Sparkish Gad no, madam. You will learn I go to a play as I go to a country picnic. I carry my wine to one and my wit to the other or else I'm sure I would not be merry at either.

Alithea (*singing*) Why did he have to come into my life
Turning my world around
Filling my heart with dreams that can't be
Turning my world around
Upside down.

Sparkish Pox, where are the sedan chairs? If we don't hurry we'll miss Captain Jack. Alithea, wait here with Harcourt. I'll see if I can find them.
Pinchwife I'll go with you, Sparkish. It's time I returned to my ailing wife. Good-night, sister. Harcourt, I'll see you tomorrow at the canonical hour.
Sparkish (*as he exits with Pinchwife*) Now about the dowry, Pinchwife ...

They exit

Alithea (*singing*) Why does he smile the way he smiles
Harcourt Why does she look the way she does
Both Why when I look in her/his eyes do I feel alive
Don't tell me I'm in love.

Alithea My fiancé seems to be making a habit of forcing my company upon you, sir. I apologize for the imposition.
Harcourt I assure you, madam, no apology is necessary. You must be very excited — come this time tomorrow you'll be a married lady.
Alithea Indeed, sir.
Harcourt He's a most fortunate fellow.

Both (*singing*) Why when I look in his/her eyes do I feel alive
Don't tell me I'm in love
Why did love have to come into my life
Turning my world around
Upside down.

Taking her hand, Harcourt exits with Alithea

Cross-fade to:

SCENE 7

Pinchwife's lodgings. Tuesday 6.15 p.m.

Margery is stretched out on a chaise-longue, *lost in thought*

Pinchwife enters

Margery (*jumping up*) Oh honey-bud, you're home.
Pinchwife (*smiling benignly*) How astute.
Margery Please can we take the air, honey-bud? I've been cooped up in these rooms all day.
Pinchwife Take comfort, my sweet — you shall have air enough when we return to the country on Friday.

Margery Pish the country!

Pinchwife I beg your pardon, madam?

Margery Pish! Pish! Pish the country! I want to see some sights.

Pinchwife Margery, I thought —

Margery (*interrupting*) Where's Alithea?

Pinchwife She's gone with Sparkish to see the Captain off.

Margery Then why can't we go too? I hear all London'll be there.

Pinchwife Margery —

Margery (*interrupting*) Oh please, bud, let's go before it's too late.

Pinchwife I thought perhaps we'd have an early night, dearest.

Margery But we have nothing else when we're back in Hampshire.

Pinchwife No, no. An early night.

Margery An early night?

Pinchwife An early night ... you know.

Margery looks at him blankly

(*Suggestively*) An early night.

Margery Oh ... an early night. I see. Well husband, if you won't indulge me in my little pleasures ... I'll not indulge you in yours.

Pinchwife Margery —

Margery (*interrupting*) I mean it, bud. Flat and plain.

Pinchwife You've only been here two days and already you've got the obstinacy of a town jade.

Margery But why can't I go and see the Captain off?

Pinchwife Because, idiot that you are, your admirer is bound to be there — may the pox rot his legs and spread ever upwards. Once he sees you there'll be no stopping the dog.

Margery I could always wear a mask.

Pinchwife (*derisively*) A mask ... ? A masked woman is like a covered dish: it gives a man an appetite when the same dish left uncovered would turn his stomach. No no ...

Margery In that case husband, I will have an early night.

Pinchwife (*with relief*) Margery ...

Margery (*as she goes*) On my own.

She exits

Pinchwife Wait, wait ... I have an idea ...

He exits

Cross-fade to:

SCENE 8

The quay. Tuesday 7 p.m.

Horner, Sir Jasper, Lady Fidget, Dorilant, Dainty, Sparkish, Harcourt and Alithea are talking together. There is a hubbub of noise and a festive air. A Fiddler is playing a jig

Quack enters pushing a wheelbarrow

Horner (*looking upwards; calling*) Come on, Captain! Let's be having you. We haven't got all night.
Sir Jasper We've beds to go to, sir.
Dorilant Ay, and homes to go to afterwards.

The others laugh

Sparkish Perhaps he's got cold feet.
Quack If he hasn't he soon will have.

All laugh

Horner Come on, Captain!
Harcourt (*taking Horner's arm*) Horner, a word ...
Horner It's too late to change your mind ... What is it, Harcourt?
Harcourt I need some advice concerning a lady.
Sir Jasper It's pointless asking him that!

The others laugh

Horner A maimed general, though unfit for action, is still fit for counsel, Sir Jasper. (*To Harcourt*) Communicate.
Harcourt I'm in love with a ... certain gentleman's mistress.
Horner And what are the lady's feelings on the subject?
Harcourt I haven't told her.

Horner raises his eyes to heaven

It's not that easy, Horner. How can you tell a lady you love her on the eve of her marriage?
Horner Oh for pity's sake, Harcourt. In my time I bedded brides on their wedding day.

Dainty (*coquettishly*) And the maid of honour.

Horner And the ... (*he remembers and smiles*) Oh yes ... (*He turns back to Harcourt*) You see, your trouble, lad, is you're too sensitive ... If you want my advice, tell her you love her, take her back to your lodgings and bed the wench.

Lady Fidget Really, Mister Horner!

Sparkish (*to Lady Fidget*) Sounds excellent advice to me.

Dorilant Absolutely, Harcourt. Get her out your system. If you've got an itch, scratch it.

Harcourt Sir, you confuse love with lust.

The ladies ad lib agreement. The men jeer derisively

Horner Harcourt, you follow my advice and I warrant come morning your so-called "love" will have lost its ardour.

Dorilant Ay, a lot less 'arder.

Pinchwife and Margery enter. Pinchwife has unsuccessfully attempted to disguise Margery's ample charms by dressing her as a man. She is wearing a periwig

Sparkish (*seeing them*) Strike me vitals. What on earth does Pinchwife think he's doing? He's dressed his wife as a man.

Dorilant So he has. The jealous toad's finally slipped his moorings. Come, let's torment the rogue. (*He moves to them*) Ah Pinchwife, dear friend. Come to see the Captain off, have we?

Pinchwife (*extremely apprehensive*) No, no, no. Just passing.

Horner Ah Pinchwife, who's the pretty young gentleman?

Pinchwife My ward.

Horner (*lasciviously*) I never saw anything so pretty in all my life.

Pinchwife (*trying to usher Margery away*) Come, let's away, brother.

Dorilant (*blocking his way*) Oh, your *brother*.

Pinchwife My wife's brother ... Thomas.

Horner (*looking at Margery*) That explains it — he's the very image of the lady I saw you with at the play.

Dorilant The one you told us you had fallen helplessly in love with.

Margery (*mesmerized*) Oh Jeminy.

Quack She must be very handsome if she looks like Thomas.

Horner Handsome ... ? (*To Margery*) She is a glorious creature. More beautiful beyond all things I ever beheld. (*To Pinchwife*) With respect, sir.

Margery Pray sir, don't mock me.

Dorilant Oh but sir, he speaks of your sister.

Pinchwife (*blustering*) Yes, yes, but saying she was handsome and he being like her you confused her ... him. The lad John ——
Lady Fidget Tom.
Pinchwife — Tom ...
Horner The same rose petal lips ...
Pinchwife Oh God!
Horner The same milk white alabaster skin ...
Pinchwife (*trying to leave*) Come, let's away, brother ——
Horner ... same fawnlike eyes. Am I not right, Pinchwife?
Pinchwife Come, come, lad. Your "sister" Margery is keeping supper for us.
Quack Methinks little Tom is so handsome he should not be a man.
All Mmmmm!

Song 11: "What a Handsome Little Fellow"

Horner What a handsome little fellow,
What a well-built lad.
(*He takes hold of Margery's thigh*) Take a feel of those thighs, sir.
Dorilant (*patting Margery's behind*) What a damn fine seat,
So firm and neat.
Sir Jasper 'Tis enough to bring a tear to your eye, sir.
All What a buxom little fellow,
What a robust lad.
Quack (*incredulously*) Will you look at that chest, sir.
In all my years, I must confess
I've ne'er seen a laddie so blessed, sir.

Horner }
Others } On my life, I've never seen a fella,
No, I've never seen a fella
Fit his breeches so well.
On my life, he's such a pretty fella,
Oh, what a pretty fella,
And I've never seen a fella
Fill his breeches so well.
Harcourt What a shapely leg.
Dorilant What a rounded hip.
Pinchwife (*to himself*) May a thousand ulcers gnaw away their lips!
Sir Jasper Have you ever known a laddie with a prettier smell?
Pinchwife (*to himself*) May their festering bodies burn in hell!
Come away, I say,
Come away, sir.
Others Nay, let the little man stay, sir.

Horner What a modest little fellow,
What a shy young lad.
You need taking in hand, sir.
Come walk with me
And I guarantee
That you'll soon feel a different man, sir.

All What a strapping little fellow,
What a well-built lad.

Quack But don't you find it strange, sir,
How he's so endowed in many ways,
(*He holds up the front flap of Margery's coat*)
While in others he appears short-changed, sir.

Horner } On my life, I've never seen a fella,
Others } No, I've never seen a fella
Fit his breeches so well.
On my life, he's such a pretty fella,
Oh what a pretty fella,
He's such a pretty fella,
And I've never seen a fella
Fill his breeches so well.

Harcourt What a slender neck.
Dorilant What silken locks.
Pinchwife (*to himself*) May their wedding tackle be devoured by pox!
Quack Have you ever seen a laddie with such peerless white skin?
Pinchwife (*to himself*) May a rabid dog tear them limb from limb.
(*To Margery*) Come away, I say.
Come away, sir!
Margery Nay, let the little man stay, sir.

Quack For we can't get over those ruby lips.
Dorilant That slender neck.
Sir Jasper Those rounded hips.
Harcourt Those big blue eyes.
Horner Those shapely thighs.
Margery Let's not forget my chest, sir.
Quack In all my years I must confess.
I've ne'er seen a laddie so blessed, sir.

Horner } On my life, I've never seen a fella,
Others } No, I've never seen a fella
Fit his breeches so well.

On my life, he's such a pretty fella,
Oh what a pretty fella,
He's such a pretty fella,
And I've never seen a fella
No, I've never seen a fella
Fill his breeches so well.
What a gorgeous little fella,
What a pretty lad.

Pinchwife The image of his sister.

Horner The one I love
With all my heart.
Pray remind me to her with this kiss, sir.
(*He kisses her*) And this, sir.
(*He kisses her*) And this, sir.

Others (*kissing her hands, arms, etc.*) And this, and this, and this and this.

Horner Remind me to your sister.

All The one he loves
With all his heart.

Horner Pray remind me to her with this ...

Others (*with a long crescendo*) Aaaah ——

Horner (*kissing her*) Kiss, sir!

There is a drum roll, in a crescendo

Dainty (*pointing upwards*) It's Captain Jack! He's off!

There is an excited babble of voices. Everyone is cheering and waving. The lines overlap

Captain Jack and the Executioner appear on a balcony

Sir Jasper Good luck, sir!
Sparkish Enjoy your trip!
Dorilant The devil take you, Captain!
Quack Mind your step, sir!
Squeamish Here he comes!

Song 12: "Tyburn Jig"

Company Hey-ho, away you go,
Grunting like a pig.

Click your heels and spin a reel
And dance a merry jig.
We doff our caps and wish you well
As you go dancing down to hell.
With a hey-ho,
Foh-de-oh-doh
You dance the Tyburn Jig.
You dance the Tyburn ...

Captain Jack Though I am to hang for highway robbery, my true crime was cuckolding a gentleman of high office. Well, a pox on you, Lord ——

Before he can finish, the trap-door opens and Captain Jack is hanged

Company Jig!

The crowd roars its approval. Pinchwife laughs and jeers at the sport

During the commotion Horner slips away with Margery. They reappear on a balcony

Pinchwife suddenly realizes Margery is missing

Pinchwife (*looking around; frantically*) Margery ... ? Has anyone seen me wi— me little Tom?

Smiling maliciously, the crowd point to Horner and Margery on the balcony

(*Outraged*) Horner!

Horner turns and bows courteously to Pinchwife. During the song, individual lights pick out the singers

Song 13: "Wait and See"/"Lust" (Reprise)

All Will she succumb to his advances?
Horner Most assuredly.
Pinchwife Will I prevent him violating my wife Margery?
All The only way you'll learn the answers to these questions,
Is to wait and see.
Wait and see.

Sparkish Will Harcourt steal the heart and hand of sweet Alithea?
Harcourt Or will it be my rival Sparkish who will marry her?
Company The only way you'll learn the answers to these questions,
Is to wait and see.
Wait and see.
Yes, you must wait and see.
Yes, you must wait and you must see.

Quack Will Jasper learn there's more to Horner than he thinks there is?

Lady Fidget
Dainty
Squeamish } Will we be caught indulging in our infidelities?

Company The only way you'll learn the answers to these questions,
Is to wait and see.
Wait and see.
Yes, you must wait and see.
You must wait and see.
We leave you now, with your permission,
For the custom'ry intermission.
So whet your whistles then return to us,
For an act brimful
Of saucy and sinful,
Good old-fashioned,
Earthy and robust
Lust!

Don't miss the act of robust lust!
Don't miss the act of robust lust!
Lust, lust,
Lust, lust,
Lust, lust, lust, lust,
Lust, lust, lust, lust,
Don't miss the act of robust lust!

Black-out

CURTAIN

ACT II

Scene 1

Various locations. Wednesday 10.45 a.m. Quack has placed Captain Jack's body in the wheelbarrow

Song 14: "Lust" (Reprise)

Quack Though it is only fifteen minutes
Since you saw us last,
Within the context of the play
More than twelve hours have passed.
And during which time much has happened
So dear patrons, without more ado,
I'll enlighten you.
Friend Horner freed of all restraint
Was like a man possessed,

The Lights pick out a clump of bushes

Passed from liaison to liaison
Hardly taking breath.
And Lady Fidget, Mistress Squeamish
And young Dainty
They were much impressed.

Horner With my zeal and zest.

Squeamish's head appears in the bushes. Horner's head appears behind her

Squeamish Sweet sir, I'm much impressed.
(*Getting carried away*) Oh yes, oh yes,
Oh yes, oh yes, oh

Both Ye-e-e-e-s!

The Lights fade on bushes. The Lights come up in the Pinchwifes' lodgings

Pinchwife, in his shirt sleeves, can be seen questioning Margery. She is still in the boy's costume

Quack And so to Pinchwife who, beside himself with jealousy,
Has for the last three hours questioned his wife Margery.

Pinchwife (*speaking*) Once more: what happened when you were alone with Horner?

Margery (*wearily*) But I've told you a thousand times.

Pinchwife Again!

Quack For if her tale should deviate with repetition
Then it is false you see.
And so too is she.
As false as false can be.
If it should deviate then she is false you see.

The Company appear in various locations, looking out of windows, etc. Quack exits with the wheelbarrow

Company So join us now for the conclusion
Of this tale of disillusion.
Of smould'ring passions,
The cut and thrust
Of an act that's brimful
Of saucy and sinful,
Good old-fashioned
Earthy and robust
Lust.
Sit back, enjoy this act of lust.
Sit back, enjoy this act of lust.
Lust, lust,
Lust, lust,
Lust, lust, lust, lust,
Lust, lust, lust, lust.
Sit back, enjoy this act of lust.

The Lights fade on the other locations, increasing on Pinchwife's lodgings

Pinchwife Once more, what did he do to you when you were alone?

Margery (*dreamily*) He kissed me a hundred times and told me he imagined he was kissing my fine sister — meaning *me* ... you know, who he said he loved with all his soul ——

Pinchwife (*interrupting*) Yes, yes, but you let slip he did some beastliness to you. Now for the last time what was it?
Margery He — he put his ... (*she falters*)
Pinchwife What? He put his what where?
Margery The tip of his tongue between my lips!
Pinchwife (*shuddering with revulsion*)An eternal canker seize the dog! Go and fetch pen, ink and paper.
Margery (*as she goes*) Yes, bud.

She exits

Pinchwife 'Tis plain she loves him. (*Bitterly*) Love! 'Twas love that gave women their art of deceiving. Out of nature's hand they came open, stupid and fit for slaves as God in heaven intended, but damned love ... Well, I'll strangle that little devil Cupid.

Music begins under the following

Margery enters with pen, paper and ink

Pinchwife Come, minx: take a letter to Mister Horner.
Margery (*sitting; excitedly*) Oh Lord.
Pinchwife Begin. Dear Sir ...
Margery Shouldn't I say, "Dear Mr Horner"?
Pinchwife Write!
Margery (*writing*) Dear Sir ...
Pinchwife Though last night I suffered your nauseous kisses and embraces ——
Margery (*interrupting*) But he had the sweetest breath.
Pinchwife (*threatening*) Write!
Margery Couldn't I leave out "nauseous", honey-bud?
Pinchwife Write as I bid you, or by God I will put out your eyes and carve "whore" across your forehead.
Margery (*writing*) Yes, honey-bud.

Song 15: "Dear Sir"

Pinchwife (*vehemently*) Dear Sir ...
No, make that plain "Sir".
Margery (*writing; dreamily*) My dear sweet Mister Horner
Pinchwife Though last night I suffered your nauseous
Kisses and embraces

Margery (*writing*) How I hunger for your glorious
Kisses and embraces
Pinchwife Wait! Add "odious" to "nauseous"
Margery Add "heavenly" to "glorious"
Both Kisses and embraces.
Pinchwife You should not construe that I'm in anyway attracted to you, sir.
In fact, no-one else revolts me as you do, sir.
Margery (*writing*) I'll never weary of the sight of you, sir.
Pinchwife (*warming to his task*) Good, good.
Excellent, excellent.
Continue as I bid you, madam, write!
I'm sickened by your very sight.
Margery I hunger for you ev'ry night.
Pinchwife You're nothing but a libertine.
Margery Your image fills my ev'ry dream.
Pinchwife A canker on the human race.
Margery I'm haunted by your sweet embrace.
Pinchwife I abhor you.
Margery I adore you.
Pinchwife I despise you.
Margery Idolize you.
Both But nothing that I write can do
Justice to the way I feel for you, sir.
Pinchwife Good, good.
Excellent, excellent.
Continue as I bid you ...
Margery Pray allow me to finish, husband, wait!
(*Writing*) Dear, sir,
There's just one thing, sir ...
Pinchwife (*gloating*) I can't wait to see his smug face
Margery I must ask you to appear devious
When you read this letter.
Pinchwife It'll make that smug dog nauseous
When he reads this letter.
Margery Wait,
Not devious, it's dolorous
Pinchwife Quite nauseous and bilious
Both When you read/he reads this letter.
Margery It would never do to let my husband learn my feelings for you, sir.
For I swear that he would kill me if he knew, sir.

Pinchwife Your nemesis is way long overdue, sir!
(*To Margery*) Finished?
Margery Finished.
Pinchwife Excellent, excellent.
Now sign it plain and simply, madam ...
Both Yours,
Margery (*writing frantically*) To command till death,
Your ever loving and devoted servant who ...
Pinchwife Missus
Margery Misses your sweet kisses
And who, if doesn't see you soon will end her life
Both Margery Pinchwife
Margery (*writing*) Kiss, kiss. (*She seals the letter*)

Black-out

The Lights come up on Quack

Quack While the letter wings its merry way
We find its recipient, our bird of prey,
Reclining in his chamber, languidly replete,
From sampling the pleasures of a "dainty" treat.

Cross-fade to:

Scene 2

Horner's lodgings. Wednesday 11 a.m.

A large four-poster bed dominates the room. An extremely smug Horner is preening himself in a mirror

A breathless, dishevelled Dainty is sitting on the bed buttoning up her bodice

Dainty Was it really glorious for you?
Horner (*bored*) Glorious.
Dainty And you truly heard angels sing?
Horner At the tops of their voices.
Dainty And bells ringing?
Horner Bells ... It was deafening.

Church bells chime. Realizing Lady Fidget is due, Horner collects Dainty's clothes

Dainty And the earth ——

Horner (*interrupting*) Moved ... moved.

Dainty (*crossing*) I feel so honoured ... To think you suffered the greatest shame that could befall a man just so no hint of shame might fall on me.

Horner Your reputation is paramount in my eyes, Mistress — er — Mistress ...

Dainty Dainty.

Horner Dainty. Paramount. Same time tomorrow, madam?

Dainty I count the hours, sir.

Horner (*taking a phallic-shaped vase from the chest at the foot of the bed*) If anyone asks, you've been out buying china. (*He holds the vase suggestively to his loins*) And remember: not a word of our little secret.

Dainty (*clasping the vase to her breast*) Not even if they pulled out my fingernails, ripped out my tongue, gouged my eyes ——

Horner (*interrupting*) Yes, yes, splendid. I get the gist. Close the door after you, Mistress Paramount.

Dainty Dainty.

Horner Ah, Dainty ... of course, yes.

Quack enters

Quack (*as he enters*) Horner, I ——

Dainty I've been out buying china. I've been out buying china. (*As she exits*) I've been out buying china.

The flustered Dainty scurries past Quack and exits

Horner She's been out buying china.

Quack I was inquisitive to know whether your strategy was working. It appears the question has been answered.

Horner My assumption was correct, dear Quack. These so-called women of virtue, like their brothers in religion, fear the eye of society more than the eye of the Almighty.

There is a conspiratorial tap on the door

Lady Fidget (*off; half-whispered*) Mister Horner?

Quack Another? Already?

Horner (*smirking knowingly*) If you'll excuse me ...

Quack Perhaps I could — er — step behind the screen and see for myself what particular privileges you have with these so-called "women of virtuous reputation".

Horner If you must. Personally, I find watching another in the throes of passion is about as enjoyable as counting another man's money.

Quack (*stepping behind a screen*) Really? I've always found it most stimulating myself.

There is another conspiratorial tap on the door. Horner leans languidly against the screen

Horner (*calling out*) Next — er — enter.

Lady Fidget enters and, seeing Horner, goes weak at the knees

Lady Fidget (*with suppressed passion*) Well Horner, am I not a woman of honour? As you see I am as good as my word.

Horner And you, madam, are about to discover that I am as good as mine.

Lady Fidget crosses to Horner and starts kissing him passionately. Horner, remaining cool and impervious to her ever-growing passion, demonstrates his skill to Quack. He runs his fingers expertly over Lady Fidget's back and neck. Pin-pointing various erogenous zones, he applies pressure which transports her ladyship to a state of near ecstasy. As she breaks away, Quack peeps leeringly from behind the screen. Horner hurriedly pushes him back

Lady Fidget But first you must promise to take care of my dear honour.

Horner One more word of honour madam, and you will make me incapable of wronging it.

Lady Fidget (*kissing his neck*) You cannot blame a woman of unsullied reputation for being ... for being ... (*she gasps*) Oh my God, that's wonderful ... for being ... for being cautious.

Horner Cautious? Dear lady, I have been cautious in the extreme already by the report I made of myself for your good sake.

Lady Fidget throws Horner on to the bed

Lady Fidget (*kissing his chest*) One cannot be too careful. (*She rips open his shirt*) Oh my God, sir, you're magnificent. Magnificent ... I followed your instructions and told my Lord Jasper that I'm gone in search of a piece of china.

Horner (*disengaging himself*) Then to work, madam, and let us see what treasures we can uncover.

They dance together

Song 16: "Ode to the One I Love"

One glance from those dazzling eyes
And it comes as no surprise

Quack peers above the screen, tosses up the jar of walnuts and sinks from sight, shaking them like maracas

That there are very few,
If any, who
Can resist you.
Your body is beyond compare,
Ruby lips and lustrous hair.
So pleasing to the eye,
It's easy to see why
They can't resist you.

Horner glances at himself in the mirror

But enough of me.
It's time I turned my attention
To you, my lady.
Prepare yourself

Horner throws Lady Fidget on to the bed

For love!

With a bound Horner leaps on to the bed and stands astride her, his back to the audience, arms akimbo. With a flourish Lady Fidget pulls down his breeches and grabs his tackle

At that moment Sir Jasper enters

Sir Jasper (*shocked*) Madam!

Lady Fidget and Horner stare at him, dumbstruck

Is this how you buy china?

Pause

Explain yourself!

Quack (*from behind the screen*) Keep a tight grip, m'lady.

Quack comes from behind the screen. He has removed his coat and rolled up his sleeves

(*Breezily*) Ah, Sir Jasper. Just changing the poor fellow's dressing.

Sir Jasper (*confused*) Dressing?

Quack (*peering at Horner's crotch*) Perfect. The swelling will go down presently, I warrant. (*To Sir Jasper*) Your lady wife came to acquire a piece of china from Mister Horner and ended up seconded into the medical profession as my assistant. (*To Lady Fidget*) You may take your hand away now, madam.

Sir Jasper Dressing?

Horner gets up, holding up his breeches

Horner (*indicating crotch*) Yes — er — yes ... dressing. (*He scurries behind the screen*)

A flustered Lady Fidget gets off the bed

Sir Jasper Oh I see. Dressing. Yes, yes, of course. Well done, m'dear. Well done. (*To Quack*) Astonishing woman. She'll put her hand to anything.

Horner reappears

Quack With an extraordinary knowledge of anatomy. Come now, Horner, you can't disappoint the lady, especially after she has been so obliging. She must have what she came for. Right, Sir Jasper?

Sir Jasper Oh, indeed, sir. I insist.

Lady Fidget Mister Horner's finest piece (*she indicates the door*) is in there. And I mean to have it.

Horner Oh, well — er — in that case if you'll ex——

Before he can finish, Lady Fidget drags him through the door

Quack I see your wife has acquired a sudden passion for porcelain.

Sir Jasper Yes, yes, it's the latest vogue, don't y'know ... My associates tell me their wives are just as bad ... Can't get enough of the damned stuff.

Quack I take it you don't share your wife's interest in china.

Sir Jasper Oh definitely not, sir ... Bit of a sore point, really. Though in my defence... (*he sings*)

Song 17: "China"

I do my damnedest to oblige her,
Try and give her a bit whenever I possibly can.
But she merely laughs and pushes it aside, sir,
And declares, sir,
Compared, sir,
To what she picks up in town, sir,
My bric-a-brac is less than grand.
She says not only aren't my off'rings
Substantial ...

Quack Ungrateful pest.
Sir Jasper But grow less frequent with each passing year.
Quack You do your best.
Sir Jasper She swears if they get any smaller
My little knick-knacks will quite disappear.
Quack To keep your lady satisfied, sir,
She needs an army to supply her.

Horner appears at a window beside the door

Horner With all modesty I disagree, sir.
I'll think you'll find, sir,
With my piece of china,
Your dear lady wife, sir,
Will be satisfied.

Lady Fidget's legs appear either side of Horner's head. He sinks out of view

Quack
Sir Jasper } China, china.
Sir Jasper She's besotted with this latest fashion.
Quack
Sir Jasper } China, china.

Sir Jasper 'Tis her greatest love and passion.
Quack Yes your lady of quality
Can never ever get enough.
Sir Jasper 'Tis true,
'Tis truly true,
She can never ever get enough.

Horner and a flushed Lady Fidget appear at the window

Horner Your wife is a true connoisseur, sir,
And as such a most difficult woman to satisfy.
Sir Jasper But by those flushed cheeks
And twinkle in her eye, sir,
I deduce, sir,
In truth, sir,
While rifling through your drawers, sir,
She's come across a major find.

Lady Fidget peers round the door

Lady Fidget You are correct, sir, in your assumption.
Sir Jasper (*to Horner*) I told you so.
Lady Fidget Mister Horner's piece is truly divine.
Sir Jasper I always know.
Lady Fidget I knew from the moment I saw it,
I'd never rest until it was mine. (*She stands in the doorway*)
Sir Jasper To make my lady so possessive,
Your piece, sir, must be most impressive.

The neck of a phallic-shaped vase, identical to the one Horner gave Dainty, slides into view from around the door

Horner In all modesty I must agree, sir.

Lady Fidget takes the vase

There is none finer
Than my piece of china,
In all London Town, sir,
'Tis truly unique.

The Lights come up on various locations to reveal Ladies fondling pieces of china identical to the piece Horner gave Dainty and Lady Fidget

All China, china.

Sir Jasper
Quack
Horner } She's besotted with this latest fashion.
All China, china.
Ladies 'Tis our greatest love and passion
And we ladies of quality
Can never ever get enough.
Sir Jasper 'Tis true,
Quack 'Tis truly true,
Horner They can never ever get enough.

All China, china, china.
Ladies We have it everywhere.
Horner On the banquet table,
Quack Half-way up the stairs.
Horner (*to Lady Fidget*) You have it in the boudoir,
Lady Fidget We have it in the hall.
Sir Jasper My wife's been known to have it
Hanging on the wall!

All China, china.
Sir Jasper
Quack
Horner } They're such dedicated followers of fashion
All China, china.
Ladies 'Tis our greatest love and passion.
And we ladies of quality
Can never ever get enough.

Men 'Tis true,
'Tis truly true,
They can never ever get
Ladies Never ever get,
All Never ever get enough.
Never never ever get enough.

Lady Fidget and Sir Jasper exit

Horner (*laughing*) Quack, you are a genius. How can I ever repay you?

Quack (*laughing*) The look on your face was payment enough, Horner. It'll be with me till the day I die. There you were, breeches at half-mast, cannon primed and ready for action.

Horner Lady Fidget positioned to take a broadside.

Pinchwife enters

Pinchwife Horner!

Horner Pinchwife, dear friend.

Pinchwife (*smugly; handing him the letter*) A letter, "dear friend".

Horner opens it

Horner (*taken aback*) But this is from your wife.

Pinchwife Correct.

Horner reads with growing astonishment.

(*Gloating*) You looked surprised, sir. Did you expect a kinder letter?

Horner No, no; faith, how could I?

Pinchwife I thought perhaps after last night when you kissed and courted my wife ——

Horner (*interrupting; indignantly*) Last night? I assure you, Pinchwife, I did no such thing. I've never seen your wife except at the play.

Pinchwife Do not take me for an arrant fool, sir! Last night.

Horner Last night?

Pinchwife Last night at the hanging.

Horner The hanging?

Quack You mean — (*to Horner*) Good grief! Little Tom was his wife!

Horner His wife!

Pinchwife Well, as you can see it was to no avail, Horner. She despises you. Your kisses turned her stomach.

Horner hands the letter to Quack, who reads it

Horner Pinchwife, once and for all I have no designs on your wife.

Pinchwife Well, I care not one way or the other. Her letter makes her feelings perfectly clear.

Horner You seem to be unaware, sir, that I am sadly depleted.

Pinchwife Your financial tribulations are no concern of mine, sir. (*As he goes*) I bid you good-day.

Pinchwife exits

Horner (*calling after him*) Pinchwife ...
Quack (*handing back the letter*) Granted the creature's willing, but Pinchwife is so rabidly jealous and watches her so closely that I fear her desires will remain forever on the page and not in your bed.
Horner It's not Pinchwife's vigilance that concerns me, Quack, it's time. Time. They leave for the country immediately after the wedding. If I had four days I could breach his defences, but four hours ...

The Lights fade isolating Horner and Quack

Quack (*singing*) It's a fact of human nature you can be sure,
When something's unobtainable you crave it more.

Horner I must have her Quack. I must have her.

Quack (*singing*) A statement that is proved, as you will see,
By the pitiful state of Harcourt, Alithea, Horner and Margery.

The Lights cross-fade to reveal:

Scene 3

Pinchwife's lodgings immediately after. Wednesday 11.30 a.m. Music continues under the following

There is a stack of walking sticks by the door

Margery is seated at a table writing a letter

Margery Dear, dear, dear Mister Horner. (*She stops writing and sighs*) It seems I have caught the disease they call love. It is just like malaria, for when I think of my husband I tremble and have inclinations to vomit. But when I think of my dear sweet Mister Horner I grow hot and am consumed by fever. For in his chamber I warrant I'd find the remedy to my *malaise* ... I must be with him. I must. (*She starts writing*)

Spots pick out Harcourt and Alithea on opposite sides of the stage

Song 18: "Come Tomorrow"

Harcourt Come tomorrow she'll be gone.
And with her goes my heart.
Come tomorrow she'll be gone
And loneliness will start.
Alithea Seems I've known him all my life
Although it's just a day.
Seems I've known him all my life,
How can I walk away.

Margery
Harcourt
Alithea
Now I'll never be your lover.
Speak the words I long to say.
Never taste your soft sweet kisses
And in your arms I'll never lay.
Harcourt Never feel her warm beside me.
Alithea Whisper words that lovers know.

Harcourt
Alithea
Never wake to find you sleeping
In morning's pale and gentle glow.
Harcourt Come tomorrow she'll be gone.
Alithea Come tomorrow he'll be gone.
Margery Come tomorrow he'll be gone.
Harcourt And with her goes my heart.
Alithea And with him goes my heart.
Margery And with him goes my heart.

Margery
Harcourt
Alithea
Come tomorrow he'll/she'll be gone
And loneliness will start.
And loneliness will start.

The Lights fade on Alithea and Harcourt

Unnoticed by Margery, Pinchwife enters and snatches up the letter

Pinchwife What is this?
Margery Oh Lord!
Pinchwife (*reading*) "Dear, dear, dear Mister Horner. If you love me as I love you you will not suffer me to lie in the arms of a man I loathe and detest. Therefore I beseech you, free me from this unfortunate match

before this afternoon or else, alas, I shall be forever out of your reach. For I can defer no longer our ... (*he looks up*) Our what? Our journey into the country, I suppose? Come, harlot, write! What was to follow "our"? (*He crosses to the stack of walking sticks*)

Margery looks around desperately

(*He measures a stick for thickness against his thumb*) The rule of thumb, madam. The rule of thumb. The law permits a husband to beat his deceiving, cheating, hussy of a wife as long as the stick is no thicker than his thumb ... Then again, who's to know? (*He crosses with the stick*) Now madam, write. What was to follow "our"?

Margery writes frantically for a moment

Margery (*handing him the letter*) There.
Pinchwife (*reading*) "... for I can defer no longer our wedding. Your slighted Alithea ...?"
Margery It was she who made me write the letter and told me what to write.
Pinchwife Alithea? But she's to marry Sparkish before the day's out.
Margery It's the truth, bud. I swear on my mother's life.
Pinchwife But why would she make you write a letter when she can write herself?
Margery Why ...? (*Flustered*) Because ... because ... (*With sudden inspiration*) Because if Mister Horner refused her and showed others the letter she could disown it, the hand not being hers.
Pinchwife So Horner merely pursued you as a decoy.
Margery Yes.
Pinchwife (*laughing*) The cunning fox. (*Angrily*) God's death, this is inexcusable — the shameless trollop's promised to Sparkish. Come, madam, where is my sister?
Margery In her room, crying. 'Tis most pitiful to hear.
Pinchwife (*moving to exit*) Then I must speak with her.
Margery (*flustered*) No, honey-bud, wait ... Let me speak with her first and tell her that I've told you. She'll kill me otherwise. Please.
Pinchwife Oh very well, but tell her to come down.
Margery (*as she moves to the landing*) Yes, dearest.
Pinchwife Wife, sister ... sister, wife ... names that conjure up visions of love and duty, pleasure and comfort, but in reality bring nothing but plague and torment.

During the following dialogue, Margery is seen changing into Alithea's clothes

Margery (*calling from the landing*) Alithea says she will only come down if you promise to take her straight to Mister Horner, whom she tells me promised her marriage.

Pinchwife Did he now? Promise her marriage? Well you can inform my sister, madam, Mister Horner will never be part of this family. Never, I 'gad that she could even consider him above Sparkish beggars belief. Not only is the man a debauched, womanizing lecher, but his stock is far inferior to Sparkish's. Far inferior.

Margery But if that be so, honey-bud, couldn't you reduce the dowry?

Pinchwife What? Reduce the dowry?

Margery Considerably.

Pinchwife I could? (*To himself*) Indeed I could. (*To Margery*) And — er — she is certain the rogue promised her marriage?

Margery Ay, on that she's most emphatic.

Pinchwife Then tell her to come down and I will take her to him immediately.

Margery The thing is, honey-bud, she's that ashamed she cannot bear to look you in the face. Therefore, I told her to wear a mask.

Pinchwife A mask?

Margery The poor creature's so upset, honey-bud. Please.

Pinchwife Oh, very well, tell her to come down here.

Margery exits

I swear it's as much trouble getting someone to bed your sister as it is stopping them from tumbling your wife. At all events, I'd rather be Horner's brother-in-law than his cuckold.

Margery, masked and wearing Alithea's hooded cloak, enters

Ah, there you are, sister. (*He takes her arm*) Come along, come along. (*He calls*) I'll be back presently, Margery.

Margery reveals her face from behind the mask when Pinchwife isn't looking

They exit

As the Lights fade, a spot picks out Quack

Quack Though Pinchwife may appear like a blind old fool,
His foolishness is one inherent in us all.
For remember, there are none so blind as he
Who only sees that which he wishes to see.

The Lights come up to reveal:

Scene 4

Horner's lodgings. Wednesday 12 noon

Horner is lounging on his bed, smoking a hookah and reading Margery's letter

Horner (*singing*)London's fair and crowded streets
Once held me in their spell
But now I've found they've lost their charms
Bore me more than I can tell

Quack enters

Quack What! Not so much as one virtuous lady of quality?
Horner No more than a short respite, I fear.
Quack What's wrong, sir? You seem somewhat melancholy.
Horner I don't know ... things seem to have lost their sparkle.
Quack What has?
Horner Well, everything. (*He drops the letter on the bed*)

Quack picks up the letter and reads it

Song 19: "A Little Time in the Country"

Horner Spicy foods and sauces rich
Once filled me with delight.
But now they make my stomach turn
And I've lost me appetite.
Quack If you want my professional advice ——
Horner How much?
Quack I'll give it to you free.
What you crave is to sup on more wholesome fare
Only found in the country.
Only found in the country.

There's nothing as sweet as an English pear,
Juicy and ripened in the summer sun,
Freshly plucked from a neighbour's tree

Horner And eaten at your leisure when the day is done.

Quack As your physician it's plain to see
You need to spend a little time

Both A little time, a little time,
You need to spend a little time in the country.

Quack Hidden vales.

Horner (*sighing*)Ah ...

Quack Perfumed nooks.

Horner (*sighing*)Ah — ooh ...

Quack Drinking your fill
From some secret brook.
Plump young fruit.

Horner (*sighing*)Ahh ...

Quack Firm and ripe.

Horner (*sighing*)Mmm ...

Quack Opened to reveal nectareous delights.

Horner Nectareous delights?

Quack Nectareous delights.
Opened to reveal

Both Nectareous delights.

Horner With your prognosis
I must agree.
I need to spend a little time

Both Little time, little time,
Need to spend a little time
In the country.

Quack If Margery Pinchwife were more astute.
Crafty, canny, or connivingly cute.

Horner A little more intelligent,
Then I'm bound,
I could spend a little time,

Both Little time, little time.
You could spend a little time
In the country,
Without leaving London Town.
For some hey and some ho and some foh de oh dee.

There is a knock at the door

Pinchwife (*off*) Horner.
Horner / **Quack** (*together*) Pinchwife?
Horner (*calling out*) Come.

Pinchwife enters with Margery

Pinchwife Last time, sir, I brought you a letter. Now you see a mistress.
Quack (*to Horner*) A mistress? How obliging. (*To Pinchwife*) But on your word as a gentleman, sir, is she clean?
Pinchwife (*outraged*) Clean? You take her for a whore? I'll have you know, she is a relation of mine!
Horner (*to Quack*) Then he is even more obliging. (*To Pinchwife*) Alas sir, however, I have no use for her.
Pinchwife That's not what I was informed, sir. According to the lady you promised her marriage.
Horner (*taken aback*) Marriage? Good God, sir! I can assure you, Pinchwife, I have done no such thing. (*He turns to Margery*) Now madam ...

Margery whispers to Horner

(*To Pinchwife*) The lady wishes you to withdraw while she speaks to me in private.
Pinchwife She is unwilling, it seems, I should know all her shameless conduct in this affair. Well, I'll leave you together and hope while I'm gone you'll agree. If not, you and I, sir, will disagree. In the meantime I'll fetch a parson ... (*as he goes*) and break the news to Sparkish. Your servant, sir.

He exits

Quack (*half-whispered; to Horner*) Marriage? Parson? What the devil's going on?

Horner hushes him, taking him aside

Who is it?
Horner Our letter writer.
Quack Margery Pinchwife?

Horner It appears we underestimated Little Tom's intelligence. (*He ushers Quack out*) Now later, dear Quack, you shall be my guest for dinner, but first I must have a little time in the country.

Quack slips behind the screen

(*Pulling him out*) In private.

Quack exits

Horner closes the door and turns to Margery, who has removed her mask

Song 20: "The Master Class"

Horner Prepare yourself for love!

Horner cavorts around the bed with Margery

In the art of which I am a virtuoso.
I can sense your passion has grown intense,
So let the master class commence,
And together we'll create our own concerto.
Follow me and I guarantee
We'll scale the heights of ecstasy.

Climbing on to the bed, Horner and Margery draw the curtains around the four-poster. The rest of the song consists of increasingly excited "oohs" and "aahs"

Black-out

SCENE 5

A street. Wednesday 12.30 p.m.

The Lights come up as Alithea enters followed by Harcourt

Harcourt Alithea, wait.
Alithea No.
Harcourt Alithea, I must speak with you.
Alithea Please don't.
Harcourt You cannot go through with this marriage.
Alithea The writings have been drawn, sir, settlements made. 'Tis too late for stopping even if I wanted to. It would be unjust to him.

Harcourt Then why not to me?
Alithea I have made no obligation to you, sir.
Harcourt But you hold my love ... my heart.
Alithea I had his before.
Harcourt You cannot believe that.
Alithea If he did not love me, why would he marry me?
Harcourt Alithea, marriage to Sparkish is rather a sign of interest than love. He that marries a fortune covets a mistress, not loves her.
Alithea As he is true to me so must I be to him.
Harcourt Why must women, like fortune, only be true to fools?

Sparkish enters

Sparkish That was a very short visit you made Mister Horner, madam. No doubt when you return, the parson will have arrived to marry you.
Alithea (*confused*) Marry me ...?
Sparkish Pshaw. Could you find no country fool to abuse that you had to pick on me, a gentleman of wit and intelligence, you unworthy, false woman!
Alithea Either you have been drinking or you are deluded.
Sparkish Ay, by you.
Harcourt Explain yourself, sir!
Sparkish Explain myself? This unworthy, false woman wrote a letter to Horner and between them deluded me of his condition so I would not suspect him as a rival.
Alithea (*angrily*) That is not true!
Sparkish Madam, your brother has just this moment showed me the letter and told me to my face he'd left you at Horner's lodgings while he went to fetch a parson. Well madam, I wish you joy. Joy, joy, joy. Joy, joy, joy. And to him joy. And to myself even greater joy for not marrying you. Shall I tell you something? Shall I let you into a little secret? Yes, I never felt any passion for you 'til now and now the only passion I feel is hatred! 'Tis true I would have married you for your dowry, as I find Horner is, but for no other reason. And so to you, madam, I say pshaw! And good-day.

Sparkish exits

Alithea Mister Harcourt, I must solve this riddle — lead me to Mister Horner's lodgings.

Alithea and Harcourt exit

Red pulsing lights come up on the bed. Reprise section of "The Master Class". The Lights fade on the bed and come up on the street

Lady Fidget, Squeamish and Dainty enter

Dainty But sisters, is it proper for ladies of our standing to visit Horner's lodgings unescorted?

Squeamish After three bottles of Sir Jasper's best claret I care not a jot for propriety.

Lady Fidget Besides, if our gentlemen insist on deserting us again they can not reproach us if we seek our own amusement. Come, ladies, let us away and bait the gelding.

The Ladies exit

Red pulsing lights come up on the bed. Reprise section of "The Master Class". The Lights fade on the bed and come up on the street

Pinchwife and a Parson enter

Pinchwife No, no, Sparkish is no longer to marry Alithea. It is to be Horner.

Parson Ah, so Horner is to marry Sparkish.

Pinchwife No, no, no, no ...

Pinchwife and the Parson exit

Red pulsing lights come up on the bed. Reprise section of "The Master Class". The Lights fade on bed and come up on the street

Dorilant, Sir Jasper and Rudge enter

Dorilant I hate to ruin an otherwise enjoyable morning, but we really must collect our ladies from Horner's lodgings.

Sir Jasper Poor fellow, we take advantage of his condition unmercifully, do we not?

Rudge No more than a sultan would his eunuch, sir.

Laughing, Dorilant, Sir Jasper and Rudge exit

Red pulsing lights come up on the bed. Reprise section of "The Master Class". As the song ends, the Lights revert to normal for:

Scene 6

Horner's lodgings. Wednesday 1.00 p.m.

Horner crawls out of the bed exhausted. Margery, with boundless energy, clambers after him

Margery What? Weary of me already?
Horner No, no, no, faith. It's just that I fear it's time you returned to your husband.
Margery But I have no interest in going back to that crusty toad. You shall be my husband now.
Horner No, no, no. I cannot be your husband. You already have a husband.
Margery But every day in London I see ladies leave their husbands and go and live with other gentlemen as their wives.
Lady Fidget (*off*) Horner!
Horner Pox! It's those damn women ... And I was just getting up my second wind ... quick, madam, back to bed.
Margery You men are all alike.

Margery pulls Horner through the curtains of the bed

As Horner disappears, Lady Fidget, Squeamish and Dainty enter carrying travelling flasks

Ladies (*as they enter*) Horner ...
Horner (*in a stifled voice*) Make yourselves at home, ladies and — er — I'll ... I'll be with you presently.
Lady Fidget To be sure of our welcome, dear toad, we brought our own entertainment.
Dainty And to ensure we'll be merry, we came alone.
Squeamish A toast! Liquor, which makes our gentlemen short-sighted.

They all drink from their flasks

Lady Fidget I don't know whether it's Sir Jasper's brandy or your good company, dear friends, but I feel compelled to make you the confidantes of a little secret.
Dainty A secret?
Squeamish Oh, how exquisite!
Lady Fidget I have a lover.

Squeamish Lady Fidget ... No !
Lady Fidget Yes!
Squeamish No !
Dainty (*giggling*) Well, if the truth be told ... So have I.
Lady Fidget No!
Dainty Yes!
Squeamish And I!
Dainty }
Lady Fidget } (*together*) No!
Squeamish Yes!

They find this hugely amusing

Lady Fidget (*conspiratorially*) Let us be indiscreet and name them.
Horner (*alarmed*) No, no, madam, let us not!
Lady Fidget (*ignoring him*) Agreed?
Dainty }
Squeamish } (*together*) Agreed.
Horner Ladies, ladies, would you betray your lover's trust?
Lady Fidget I'll begin.

Horner, now dressed, appears from the bed

Horner (*desperately*) Madam —
Lady Fidget (*holding him to her bosom*) This is my false rogue.

There is a shocked silence

Squeamish Horner ...? (*To Horner*) But he said it was for my sake that he reported himself a eunuch.
Dainty Your sake? He swore it was for my love and honour!
Lady Fidget Horner, explain your conduct (*grabbing him by his shirt front and his crotch, she hoists him on to the step*) ... sir!
Horner (*lost for words*) You want me to explain? (*Thinking on his feet*) Very well, if it's an explanation you want, then an explanation you shall have. Everything I did I did for the one amongst you whom I truly love. For I knew that you, her two friends, were so censorious that if you so much as suspected our liaison you'd prejudice her honour. Therefore I prejudiced yours and by making the secret your own, ensured your silence. In short ladies, to serve my one true love I serviced you other two. But the question still remains: which of you is you? And which of you two are the other two? A clue.

Song 21: "One of You"

Horner With one of you,
Love was glorious.
The other two,
Merely laborious.
But which of you
Is you?
And which of you two,
Are the other two?

The one I love's,
A most desirous thing.
With her, I swear,
I heard angels sing
And bells ring,
Ding, dong, a-ling.
Ding, dong, a-ling.

Ladies (*to themselves*) Me, me.
It's obviously me, me.
I'm that wonderous thing,
That made angels sing.
I alone can make his bells ring.
Ding, dong, ding.
Ding, dong, a-ling.

Horner (*to himself*) With vanity like theirs
It's so easy to deceive them.
Their self-esteem
Knows no bounds.
Squeamish Take a look at that look in their eyes,
They know it's me.
Lady Fidget I can tell I'm the woman, every woman here
Yearns to be.
Dainty As a sensual *femme fatale*
I'm a paragon.
Ladies After all, half the men in London
Can't be wrong.
Can't be wrong.

Horner With one of you
Ladies (*to themselves*) That's me
Horner Love's a noble quest.
The other two
Ladies (*to themselves, looking at the other two*) That's you.
Horner More an endurance test.
But which of you,
Is you?

Ladies Me.
Horner And which of you two,
Are the other two?
Ladies I know, I know, I know he's talking about me.
Horner Which is you?
Ladies I know, I know, I know he's talking about me.
Horner } Which is you?
Ladies } Oo-oo-oo-ooh
Horner Which one is you?

Dainty Me.
Horner You.
Squeamish Me.
Horner You.
Lady Fidget Me.
Horner You.
Ladies I know, I know, I know he's talking about me.

There is a commotion off stage

Horner Ladies, it appears I have company. Remain concealed till I send them away.

Lady Fidget, Squeamish and Dainty go towards the bed

Behind the screen, behind the screen.

The dialogue takes place off stage as the Ladies hide themselves behind the screen

Pinchwife (*to Alithea*) Neither your sudden change of dress nor your emphatic denials shall persuade me I did not escort you to Horner's lodgings.

Alithea Sir, this is a damnable conspiracy against my honour.
Sparkish We will soon hear the truth, madam, when we speak to Horner.
Alithea Ay, and I'll be vindicated.

Pinchwife, Alithea, Harcourt, Sparkish and Parson enter

Margery, unnoticed, watches the following from the bed

Pinchwife Horner, did I or did I not escort my sister to these lodgings earlier?
Alithea Well sir, speak up!
Horner Ah yes, well ... I'd rather not.
Alithea And I'd rather you did, sir.
Horner Oh well ... in that case yes, Pinchwife, indeed you did.
Alithea That's preposterous.
Pinchwife (*to Alithea*) Now who's deluded, madam?
Sparkish Five thousand guineas.
Alithea (*to Harcourt*) Harcourt, I swear ——
Harcourt (*interrupting*) Trouble yourself not, madam, I believe your innocence.
Pinchwife Come, Horner. The parson's waiting.
Horner Then let Harcourt employ the fellow.
Pinchwife Harcourt?
Horner I've no use for her. I relinquish her to him. (*To Harcourt*) And — er — you have my consent.
Pinchwife (*outraged*) Well by God's blood he has not mine, sir! Now either you marry her or ... (*He starts to draw his sword*)

Margery runs between them

Margery Wait!

The Ladies pop up from behind the screen, gasp and pop down again

Pinchwife (*in disbelief*) Margery?
Alithea In my cloak!
Horner Shitese!

A spot picks out Quack. The Company freeze whenever Quack sings

Song 22: "Vengence"

Quack All the years of frustration,
Pent up humiliation
Erupted in a single word
Pinchwife Bastard!
Quack The devil took control.
Pinchwife Bastard!
Quack A lust for vengence seized his brain.
Knowing Horner had cajoled him
Into helping him cuckold him
Fairly drove the man insane.

Horner I'm nothing to your wife.
Margery But Mister Horner, that's not true.
Horner If you'll just listen I'll explain.
Pinchwife I'll not be fooled by you again.
Quack Horner passionately pleading —
Horner Sir, looks can be misleading.
Quack — Only served to fan the flame.
Horner Things aren't what they appear.
Pinchwife Explain the letter, damn your eyes.
Horner It was a ruse, sir. Nothing more.
Pinchwife I'll kill you first and then the whore.
Horner An attempt to stop the wedding
Alithea's been dreading
So she can wed her true amour.
Pinchwife Bastard!
Horner For it's Harcourt she adores.
Pinchwife }
Sparkish } You bastard!
Alithea Harcourt, amour.
Pinchwife You bastard!

Pinchwife continues attacking Horner. Horner uses Harcourt and Alithea as a shield. Harcourt and Alithea are so in love they are oblivious to everything but each other

Harcourt (*to Alithea*) Could what he said be true, dear lady?
You'd truly be my wife?
Alithea I'll cherish, honour and obey,
And love you all my life.
Pinchwife Bastard!

Harcourt Did you hear what she said, Horner?
She says that she'll be mine.
Alithea I'll cherish, honour and obey,
And love him for all time.
Harcourt And it's all because of you, Horner,
Horner What?
Harcourt Because of you.

Sir Jasper enters

Sir Jasper (*as he enters*) What's the matter, sir? What's the matter? I beseech you pray communicate.
Pinchwife This bastard's whored my wife!
Horner An unsubstantiated lie.

Pinchwife, slashing at Horner, knocks over the screen, revealing the Ladies

Pinchwife As I've no doubt he's whored yours too.
Horner I'm like her brother.
Sir Jasper Sir, it's true.
Pinchwife To think their friendship is platonic,
Makes you the most moronic
Imbecile I ever knew.
Sir Jasper (*to Horner*) Are you a lying rogue?
Quack Suspicion reared its ugly head.
Sir Jasper Pray tell the truth, sir, on your life.
Quack Doubt pierced his vitals like a knife.
Sir Jasper Was my trust in you ill-fated?
Have you communicated,
Have you *** with me wife?
Pray, sir, the truth, sir, on your life,
Have you ... (*he gives two pelvic thrusts*) ... the wife?
Quack With his eyes fixed and glaring,
And both his nostrils flaring
Sir Jasper screamed a single word.

Sir Jasper (*with a crescendo*) Ooohhh
Bastard!
Pinchwife Bastard!
Quack The devil took control.
Sir Jasper
Pinchwife } Bastard!

Company A lust for vengence seized his brain.
Knowing Horner had cajoled him
Into helping him cuckold him
Fairly drove the man insane.
The hatred and the shame,
Like tinder to a flame,
Lit a fire in his brain,
Drove him insane.

Quack sings to narrate the action

Quack Facing failure with deceit,
Thinking fast, on his feet,
Changed his strategy to retreat.
Legged it madly down the street.
The word flashed round the town,

Parson His wedding tackle's still intact.
Quack Faster than pox in a whore-house.
Dorilant / **Rudge** (*to each other*) I think I saw him with your spouse.
Quack In no time the streets were teeming
With husbands who were screaming
Company Kill the fornicating louse!
Ladies / **Men** Bastard!
Dorilant They caught him by the Rising Cock.
Dainty / **Lady Fidget** / **Squeamish** By the what?
Dorilant Rising Cock.
Dainty / **Lady Fidget** / **Squeamish** Oh Lord, they've caught him by the rising cock!
Parson A well-known tavern out by the city dock.
Quack They chased him to his room.
Pinchwife cried out
Pinchwife Let's stretch his neck.
Quack Where he was fin'ly brought to bay.
Pinchwife He's had his fun now he must pay.

Quack exits to the side room

Horner's hands are tied and a noose is placed around his neck

Company Horner struggling and kicking
Was trussed up like a chicken.
Death was just a step away.
Kill him!

Struggling, Horner is manhandled on to the bed. The noose is thrown over the top of the four-poster

Death was just a step away.
Kill him!
One step away
One step away
Kill him, kill him, kill him, kill him,
Kill him, kill him, kill him, kill him,
Kill him!

As Horner is about to be hanged, Quack bursts in from the side room, leaps on to the bed and grabs the rope

Quack (*shouting*) Stop!

Horner (*desperately*) Quack, Quack, for God's sake satisfy these gentlemen of my condition before I die for a crime I never committed ... And what is worse, the reputation of these poor innocent ladies dies with me.

Quack The man's a eunuch.

Pinchwife A what?

The Men react angrily

Quack A eunuch. Good God, man, do you honestly believe these ladies of virtue and fidelity would be seen in his company otherwise? Trust their unspotted reputations with him?

Pinchwife Do not mock me, sir, a cuckold is a mild beast!

Horner It's true, sir. Your wife is innocent. She merely came to my lodgings to see her sister's wedding ... And what she said of her love for me was but the usual innocent revenge upon a husband's jealousy. Is that not so, madam?

Pause. Lady Fidget pushes Margery forward

Margery Yes.

Pinchwife (*sarcastically*) And I suppose you performed the operation yourself.

Quack With a single snip. (*He takes out the jar of walnuts*) I carry the offending appendages with me as a constant reminder against the evils of whoring.

The Men react scornfully

Sir Jasper Well, that's settled then.

Pinchwife You may be a gullible old fool but we'll not be taken in by their lies. Let's string the bastard up!

Quack Sir, if you refused to accept the word of a gentleman and a physician perhaps you'll believe the evidence of your own eyes.

Pinchwife We'll believe no other evidence, sir.

The Men ad lib agreement

Quack Very well, in that case, Horner, withdraw to the next room and lower your britches.

Horner (*shocked*) What!

Quack (*untying Horner's hands and removing the noose from his neck*) Sir, your life's at stake. Now is no time for modesty.

Horner Quack, for God's sake ——

Quack (*interrupting*) Sir, if you're bashful, close the shutters, sit in the corner and put a sheet over your head. It's the evidence they wish to see, not your face.

Horner (*desperately*) But Quack ——

Quack Just do it.

Horner exits into the side room

(*To Pinchwife*) I hope this will put an end once and for all to your scullerous accusations. (*Calling out*) Ready, sir?

Horner (*off*) Send them in.

The Ladies and Margery are in a state of complete trepidation

Pinchwife, Sir Jasper, Dorilant and Rudge exit into the side room

Alithea Come Harcourt, let us not waste the padre's time.

As Harcourt and Alithea exit with the Parson, the Men enter and cross to the Ladies

Sir Jasper Madam. I beg you to forgive my erroneous assumptions.
Lady Fidget (*confused*) I forgive you, Sir Jasper.
Dorilant (*to Squeamish*) Likewise, madam.
Rudge (*to Dainty*) My apologies, Mistress Dainty.
Pinchwife (*to Margery*) It appears that I too have been a trifle hasty.
Margery Honey-bud.
Dorilant Madam.
Rudge Madam.

As the Men are apologizing to the Ladies, Horner enters fastening his britches

Horner (*half- whispered*) Quack, for God's sake who is that?
Quack It's Captain Jack. When I got wind of your predicament I hoisted him through the window (*he makes a snipping motion*) and did the necessary.
Sir Jasper Well dear friends, now all is finally settled, come — you must all be my guests for dinner.

All accept

Horner You must excuse me, gentlemen (*he rubs his throat*), I do appear to have lost my appetite.
Pinchwife (*to Sir Jasper*) Much to the relief of us husbands.

All laugh

Lady Fidget (*placing a hand on Horner's shoulder*) I think perhaps I'll stay and play a hand with the poor rogue ... With my lord's permission.
Sir Jasper Of course, my dear.

Horner suddenly perks up

Squeamish In that case (*she places a hand on his other shoulder*) may I also stay for a game or two?
Dorilant Of course you may.

Horner's smile fades

Dainty And I?
Rudge Indeed.

As Dainty crosses to him, Horner becomes decidedly uneasy

Margery (*to Pinchwife*) Honey-bud?
Pinchwife By all means.

To Horner's dismay, Margery joins the Ladies of Quality

The Men exit

(*To Horner; as he exits*) You'll be seeing a lot more of our ladies now, I warrant.
Horner (*nervously*) It would appear fate has deemed it so.
Sparkish (*as he exits*) Five thousand guineas.
Horner (*noticing Quack is about to leave; desperately*) Quack, there's no need for you to leave. Stay.
Quack No, no, Horner. (*He tosses him the jar of walnuts*) You've made your bed.

Quack exits

Horner Quack ... Well, ladies. Foh!
Lady Fidget So he heard angels singing, did he, ladies?
Dainty And bells ring.
Squeamish Oh yes, we mustn't forget the beau's bells.
Margery (*licentiously*) Come, ladies, be not so censorious. Now our gentlemen no longer consider the rogue a threat because of his ... condition, we can use him as he used us — and yet remain above suspicion.
Ladies Mmmm.

Song 23: "The Master Class" (Reprise)

During the song the Ladies shepherd Horner against his will to the bed. As they remove his clothing the drapes around the four-poster bed are drawn

The Lights fade until only the bed can be seen. On the final note all the Lights go out except for a spot on Horner's face peering over the top of the four-poster bed

Black-out

The Lights come up to reveal the Company on stage

Song 24: "We Thank You"/"Lust" (Reprise)

Quack And so we've reached the climax of this tale of lewd delight.

Margery
Ladies } And hope for your sakes that it's not the last one
Reached tonight.

Company All that remains for us to do is take our bow and bid you all good-night.
All good-night.
And thank you heartedly.

Quack This troupe of humble players thanks you heartedly.

Company We thank you heartedly
For joining us in celebration,
To the glorious restoration
Of the noblest urge bestowed on us.

Men Wholesome and healthy,

Ladies Frolicsome and carefree,

Men Good old-fashioned,

Company Earthy and robust
Lust!
And long may lust reign over us.
Lust!
And long may lust reign over us.
Lust, lust.
Lust, lust.
Lust, lust, lust, lust,
Lust, lust, lust, lust.
And long may lust reign over us.

Black-out. When ready, bring up Lights

CURTAIN CALL:

Company Lust!
Lust,
Join with us in celebration.
Lust,
To the glorious restoration.
Of the noblest urge bestowed on us.

Wholesome and healthy,
Frolicsome and carefree,
Good old-fashioned,
Earthy and robust
Lust!
And long may lust reign over us.
Lust!
And long may lust reign over us.
Lust, lust,
Lust, lust,
Lust, lust, lust, lust,
Lust, lust, lust, lust,
And long may lust reign over us!

Black-out

CURTAIN

FURNITURE AND PROPERTIES LIST

PROLOGUE
Scene 1

On stage: Nil

Personal: **Quack:** staff

Scene 2

On stage: Pincers with tooth for **Quack**

ACT I
Scene 1

On stage: Nil

Personal: **Quack:** glass jar containing two pickled walnuts

Scene 2

Personal: **Dorilant:** coin

Scene 3

Off stage: Drinks (**Wench**)

Personal: **Harcourt:** glass jar (as before)
Horner: cane

Scene 4

On stage: Comb for **Margery**

Scene 5

On stage: Deck of cards
Money

Personal: **Squeamish:** fan

SCENE 6

On stage: Nil

SCENE 7

On stage: *Chaise-longue*

SCENE 8

On stage: Gallows and noose

Off stage: Wheelbarrow (**Quack**)

ACT II
SCENE 1

On stage: Wheelbarrow

Off stage: Pen, inkwell and paper (**Margery**)

SCENE 2

On stage: Large four-poster bed with draperies
Mirror
Screen
Chest containing phallic-shaped china vase

Off stage: Many phallic-shaped vases (**Horner** and **Ladies**)
Letter (**Pinchwife**)

Personal: **Quack:** glass jar (as before)

SCENE 3

On stage: Stack of walking sticks
Pen, inkwell and paper for **Margery**

SCENE 4

On stage: As for Act II, Scene 2
Hookah

Scene 5

On stage: As before

Off stage: Travelling flasks (**Ladies of Quality**)

Scene 6

Off stage: Rope and noose (**Men**)

Personal: **Pinchwife:** sword
Quack: glass jar (as before)

LIGHTING PLOT

PROLOGUE, SCENE 1

To open: Bring up spot on **Quack** in front of the tabs

Cue 1 **Quack:** "The Restoration has begun." (Page 1)
Bring up backlighting on **Company**

Cue 2 **Quack** clicks his fingers (Page 1)
Bring up to full

Cue 3 **Horner:** "Damn!" (Page 4)
Fade to single spot on **Horner**

PROLOGUE, SCENE 2

To open: Bring up surgery effect

No cues

ACT I, SCENE 1

To open: Cross-fade to orangery effect

Cue 4 **Quack** exits (Page 11)
Fade to spot on **Horner**

Cue 5 Song 4 ends (Page 12)
Black-out

ACT I, SCENE 2

To open: Bring up London street effect

No cues

ACT I, SCENE 3

To open: Bring up tavern effect

Cue 6 **Pinchwife** exits (Page 20)
Fade to spot on **Horner** *and* **Quack**

Cue 7 Song 6 ends (Page 20)
Black-out

ACT I, Scene 4
To open: Bring up interior effect (Page 21)

Cue 8 **Margery:** "Oh Jeminy." (Page 26)
Black-out

ACT I, Scene 5
To open: Bring up interior effect

Cue 9 The **Ladies** and **Horner** exit (Page 32)
Black-out. Flash of lightning. Bring up spot on **Quack**

Cue 10 **Quack:** "I warn husbands to beware." (Page 32)
Bring up spots on singers

Cue 11 **Quack:** "Husbands take care." (Page 33)
Spot on **Horner** *and* **Squeamish** DL

Cue 12 **Dorilant** exits (Page 33)
Spot on **Dainty** DR

Cue 13 **Horner** exits (Page 34)
Spot on **Lady Fidget** DC

ACT I, Scene 6
To open: Bring up exterior effect. Evening

No cues

ACT I, Scene 7
To open: Bring up interior effect

No cues

ACT I, Scene 8
To open: Bring up quay effect. Evening

Cue 14 Song 13 begins (Page 44)
Spots on individual singers

Cue 15 Song 13 ends (Page 45)
Black-out

ACT II, Scene 1
To open: Bring up general exterior effect

Cue 16 **Quack:** "Was like a man possessed ..." (Page 46)
Spot on clump of bushes

Cue 17 **Horner** and **Squeamish**: "Ye-e-e-e-s!" (Page 46)
Cross-fade to interior effect on **Pinchwife's** *lodgings*

Cue 18 **Quack:** "... then she is false you see." (Page 47)
Bring up spots on various locations

Cue 19 **Company:** "... enjoy this act of lust." Last time (Page 47)
Fade spots; increase on **Pinchwife's** *lodgings*

Cue 20 **Margery** seals the letter (Page 50)
Black-out. When ready, bring up spot on **Quack**

Cue 21 **Quack:** "Pleasures of a 'dainty' treat." (Page 50)
Cross-fade to **Horner's** *lodgings*

Cue 22 **Horner:** "'Tis truly unique." (Page 56)
Bring up lights in various locations

Cue 23 **Horner:** "... but four hours ..." (Page 59)
Fade to isolate **Horner** *and* **Quack**

ACT II, Scene 3
To open: Cross-fade to interior effect

Cue 24 **Margery:** "I must be with him. I must." (Page 59)
Spots on **Harcourt** *and* **Alithea**

Cue 25 Song 18 ends (Page 60)
Fade on **Alithea** *and* **Harcourt**

Cue 26 **Margery** and **Pinchwife** exit (Page 62)
Fade; bring up spot on **Quack**

ACT II, Scene 4
To open: Bring up interior effect; fade spot

Cue 27 Song 20 ends (Page 66)
Black-out

ACT II, SCENE 5
To open: Bring up exterior effect

Cue 28 **Alithea** and **Harcourt** exit (Page 67)
Bring up red pulsing lights on the bed

Cue 29 Reprise of "The Master Class" ends (Page 68)
Cross-fade to exterior effect

Cue 30 The **Ladies** exit (Page 68)
Repeat Cues 28 and 29

Cue 31 **Pinchwife** and the **Parson** exit (Page 68)
Repeat Cues 28 and 29

Cue 32 **Dorilant, Sir Jasper** and **Rudge** exit (Page 68)
Repeat Cue 28

ACT II, SCENE 6
To open: Revert to general interior effect

Cue 33 **Horner:** "Shitese!" (Page 73)
Spot on **Quack**

Cue 34 The drapes are drawn around the bed (Page 80)
Fade to spot on the bed

Cue 35 At the final note of Song 23 (Page 80)
Cut to tight spot on **Horner's** *face; then black-out. When ready, bring up full lighting*

Cue 36 Song 24 ends (Page 81)
Black-out

Cue 37 Curtain call (Page 81)
Bring up full lighting

Cue 38 **Company:** "And long may lust reign over us!" (Page 82)
Black-out

EFFECTS PLOT

PROLOGUE

No cues

ACT I

Cue 1 To open Scene 3 (Page 14)
Fiddle music. Fade when dialogue begins

Cue 2 To open Scene 8 (Page 39)
Fiddle music: a jig. Fade when dialogue begins

Cue 3 **Horner:** "Kiss, sir!" (Page 43)
Drum roll in a crescendo

ACT II

Cue 4 **Horner:** "... It was deafening." (Page 50)
Church bells chime